FEAR
FAITH
FACT
FANTASY

By

John A. Henderson, M.D.

2003

Parkway Publishers, Inc.
Boone, North Carolina

Also by John A. Henderson, M.D.
GOD.com:
A Deity for the New Millennium

Library of Congress Cataloging in Publication Data

Henderson, John A. (John Arthur), 1923-
  Fear, faith, fact, fantasy / by John A. Henderson.
    p. cm.
Includes bibliographical references and index.
  ISBN 1-887905-77-4
  1. God. I. Title.
  BL205 .H46 2003
  211—dc21   2003008019

Cover Design: Aaron Burleson, Spokesmedia.com

To Marie
14 Dec 03 – The day of
Saddam Hussein's capture.
Best wishes
John

FEAR   FAITH   FACT   FANTASY
is dedicated to all who do not fear God

GOD.com: A Deity for the New Millennium
was dedicated to all God-fearing people

CONTENTS

ACKNOWLEDGEMENTS

Since the publishing of *God.com – A Deity for the New Millennium* brought no threats to my life, it may be safe to recognize some who have helped and supported my efforts.

My wife, Ruth, struggled to master the computer, decipher my hand written pages, put them into manuscript form, and helps with orders, shipping, and handling. There are no words to express my appreciation, gratitude, and respect. I can only be thankful that fate placed us together when the hormones were raging. Special appreciation also goes to my computer expert son-in-law, John Ghent.

Betty Daniel, Christine Henderson, Susan Dart, the Reverend Roy Hood, and Peter Gentling M.D. made suggestions and criticisms for which I am indebted. Dr. Theodore M. Vial Jr., Associate Professor of Religious Studies, Virginia Wesleyan College, was generous with his comments and suggestions.

To our three children, their spouses, and grandchildren, I say thanks for their help and support.

PREFACE

During the time between writing my first book *God.com – A Deity for the New Millennium* and its publication, I kept thinking of more ideas to expand upon. On further study I found no logic or information that changed my thinking but I did find a large amount of illogical reasoning, contradictions, and just plain gibberish. This book contains some of the results of that study. You will note that I use the Socratic method of reasoning. I ask as many questions as I have answers.

After a reading from my first book, a woman criticized me for using the word "man" when writing about humanity, humankind, or mankind. I must confess that my critic was right and that I too have difficulty with this gender discrimination. However, I hope that I will be forgiven when I slip into the common usage of the word man and I hope to be forgiven for assigning no gender to god and no capital letter.

The World Trade Center (WTC) catastrophe of September 11, 2001, occurred after the publication of *God.com* and prompted some people to take another look at god. Many have come to realize the harm that religions and their various gods inflict upon humanity. As the French philosopher Denis Diderot noted, "The most dangerous madmen are those created by religion, and people whose aim is to disrupt society have always known how to make good use of them."

The Jewish, Christian, Muslim god (JCM god) is considered by many to be the one and only god. The concept of such a god originated at the time of Abraham and all three religions, Judaism, Christianity, and Islam, arose in the same geographic area. Most people who respect and worship this god believe that it is listening to them and keeping score on their daily activities. They believe they must answer to it for their afterlife. As a result of the World Trade Center bombings, perhaps more people will begin to question some of the beliefs concerning the JCM god.

If this book allows some readers to overcome their fear of eternal damnation by a god who does not like to be questioned or criticized, then I have succeeded. If the writings in this book allow others to realize the harmful effects of religion, I will feel even more successful. Finally, if it will give more people the courage to speak out when they hear and see the harmful effects of religion, I will be ecstatic.

I do not devote much attention to the many bibles or the many prophets of religions. The bibles are simply poorly written history books and the prophets are nothing more or less than fanatical believers or outright charlatans who are venerated by the gullible. If you study the lives and sayings of the prophets including Jesus and Muhammad, you will clearly see they had feet of clay. But this book is not about the middlemen of religion who believe they understand and communicate with god. It is about the big boss itself – the one and only god.

One must define "god" before embarking on any discussion of it. The god I am writing about is an all-knowing, all-powerful, all-righteous, and all-perfect being. This book is not about a god called Force, Energy, Love, First Cause, or Spirit. We must admit that writing about god and religion is like discussing cancer; there are hundreds of types with as many variations as there are people. You will note that I do not capitalize god throughout the book. It is a generic word and has a different meaning to all who use it.

There are many good and humane people who believe in a god and go to church. But there are many others who look at the problems of the universe and cannot believe in such a god. Most are not against a loving, compassionate, kind, forgiving god, but they are against a cruel, capricious, nitpicking, vengeful one. This book is an effort to make religion and its god more tolerant, kind, and humane. There are many who need relief from a god who requires constant adoration and praise, but will throw you into a fiery furnace and make you suffer for eternity if it is not praised and worshipped. If this book frees some readers from the guilt and dis-ease that often attends disbelief, I will feel rewarded.

Religion soars during times of crisis such as that of 9-11-01, but so does drug usage, anxiety, depression, sexual intercourse, and the purchase of chocolate. The fanatical Muslim who crashes into the World Trade Center as he screams "Allah is Great" is the same as the Catholic priest who baptized Native American babies in Peru and Mexico, then bashed their heads in so they would go to heaven while they were saved. The beliefs of Islam with its Jihad as expressed in the Koran are similar to those of Christianity as expressed by Jesus in the Bible. *(Matthew 10: 34-40)* Both threaten nonbelievers with an eternity of damnation. Both come with swords – not to bring peace on earth.

Religions and their sects need to clean up their act. Muslims, Christians, and Jews need to convince their own followers that terror and killing in the name of god will not be tolerated. They can believe what they like about heaven, hell, and immortality but murder is a no-no. The time has come for all to express their outrage at the intolerance, bigotry, fanaticism, and destruction that religions perpetrate.

GOD.com was an icebreaker. It proposed that since most people believe in god, they must want a god. I then maintained that since most want a god, humankind should create a caring, nurturing, and more feminine one. In this book, *FEAR FAITH FACT FANTASY,* I propose that man's morality and happiness do not depend upon gods, religions, vague myths, commandments, parables, and sermons. Our security and our happiness depend on our own efforts and our own ability to transcend religious myths and fanaticism.

This book can give comfort to those who no longer believe in the dogmas they were taught in childhood.

This author welcomes your views, thoughts, and discussions. Truth is difficult to reach and it can only be obtained by logic, reasoning, and verification—not by brainwashing, preaching, bribery, and threats.

WHAT IS GOD LIKE

God, according to the common definition, is an all-knowing, all-powerful, righteous, loving, and perfect being. God single-handedly created the universe, galaxies, stars, planets, life, and everything else in the universe. At all times, god knows what is going on everywhere. It is all-powerful. For example, it can bring the dead back to life. It rules the universe in a righteous, loving, and just way. God is the beginning and the end of all things in the universe. It is perfect.

We pray to and worship such a being. When we are under stress, we turn to god and pray with the hope that it will take care of us in our time of need and protect us from our enemies. God can be a comforting idea.

However, how meaningful are these attributes? In this chapter, we will discuss and analyze god's attributes.

All-Knowing god: God knows everything. Many believers maintain that god has a plan for each of us. This assertion may be true but we have no way of knowing what that plan is or how it will be implemented. However, let us consider the shattering event of September 11, 2001. A number of terrorists have been conspiring to hijack passenger airplanes and use them as missiles to destroy the World Trade Center, Pentagon, and possibly the White House. The objective of the attack is to kill thousands of people, many of whom are innocent and probably god-fearing people. The question is, "Why didn't an all-knowing god take steps to prevent such a wanton destruction?"

The September 11 attack is just one of many tragic events in human history. You may be able to recall many more where an all-knowing god could have and should have intervened to protect the innocent.

All-powerful god: An all-powerful god had the power to stop the attack on the World Trade Center. It could have exposed the conspiracy; it could have made the hijackers miss their planes; it could have, with its enormous power, stopped the planes in mid-flight, or blown them apart before hitting the World Trade Center. But the all-powerful god did none of these things. God let the attack continue and allowed thousands of people to perish, leaving behind thousands of grief-stricken children, widows, widowers, parents, and friends.

In the Christian world there is some discussion as to whether Jesus was all-powerful. If Jesus was omnipotent, he need not have died on the cross as he had the power to do whatever he wanted. Jesus committed suicide if he was all-powerful.

Perfect being: God is perfect. It is loving and it is just.

But the perfect god did not create a perfect human and it let evil enter human life. There is evil all around us. People commit robberies and murders, and they lie and cheat. We trust managers of corporations and expect them to be honest and do what is best for the stockholders in particular and society in general. Many of these managers claim to be god-fearing people, but god apparently stood aside when these god-fearing managers destroyed the livelihood of thousands of employees and shareholders.

Despite the fact that god is always depicted as a loving father, there are a number of situations which call that into question. Certainly a loving father would never torture and kill his own son to prove how loving he is.

God is jealous: It tolerates no competition. Witness the first commandment given to Moses: "Thou shalt have no other gods before me." For some believers, that commandment meant that all other gods should be destroyed – by force if necessary. This unbridled monotheism led to the deaths of thousands of nonbelievers over the centuries. So much for god's love and compassion.

The perfect loving god seems to have an unquenchable thirst for adoration. It demands that it be prayed to and worshipped constantly. It becomes angry with people who don't adore, praise, and worship it. It created a heaven for those it likes and a hell for those it doesn't like.

But there is a problem with constant adoration and praise. Imagine a small town mayor. The mayor is a perfect human being; he is loving and fair. However, to gain favors, the townspeople must endear themselves by praising him constantly; they need to beseech him with their requests for favors; they must not owe allegiance to anyone other than the mayor, and they should not belong to any rival group.

We do not call such towns wonderful places to live. We do not call such mayors fair and just. Instead, we call them corrupt and through the use of the court system and other political means, we seek to overthrow such corrupt regimes. That is because we want to retain our right of political association and the right to belong to any political group we choose. We want a rule of law, not of men. We want the mayor to do what is right without our having to beseech him, praise him, and pay tithes and bribes to him.

The demands of god are not that different from those made by the small town mayor. Americans, through their constitutional government, worked hard to get rid of such oppressive mayors and corrupt political systems. Why should we hold god to any lesser standards? God should do what is right. God should be held to the highest standards of morality and compassion. Man should not have to beg god to do what is right.

God's anger: God, the perfect being, can get mad. It became angry with mankind at one time and killed off everybody except Noah and

4

his family.   Now preachers and theologians threaten us and say it will happen again because mankind is scarred by sin.   They predict Armageddon.   In fact, they frequently predict the end of the world.   Nostradamus predicted that the end of the world would come in 3797.   William Miller predicted the world would end in 1843 and some 40,000 "Millerites" joined the movement.   1843 came and passed without incident and the believers simply changed the date.

The Scripture tells us that the sword, pestilence, and famine are god's judgments. Presumably, in modern times, god will update its arsenal to include rockets, nuclear bombs, and chemical and biological weapons.

But we must raise the questions, "How can a loving god inflict such punishment upon the good, the bad, the young, and the old, without rhyme or reason?   How can such a punishment differ from the evil perpetrated by satan, god's supposed enemy?"

God the communicator: God is a poor communicator.   It seems to prefer parables, allegories, and other indirect and ambiguous means of communication.   This leaves the door open to all who claim that they know the mind of god better than anyone else.   Certainly an omnipotent, omniscient god would not be communicating through televangelists, uneducated preachers, and charlatans.

God's commandments, supposedly absolute, are not absolute at all.   The commandment "Thou shalt not kill" is violated in thousands of ways every day.   Not just by evil people who commit murders, but by legally constituted civil societies who violate this commandment with wars, justifiable homicides, and executions. Killing is not always murder. The legal system is full of such distinctions. Just look into a thesaurus to see the many shades and nuances between the idea of murder and killing. But the commandment doesn't deal with these nuances at all, leaving the questions, "Why didn't god do a better job of defining murder and killing? Why did it risk giving such an obviously unenforceable and ambiguous command that still allows men to murder others in the name of god?" Over the centuries, the vast number of wars and holocausts that led to the murder of innocent people attest to the ineffectiveness of this command. Even the faithful, who supposedly followed god's commandments in their daily lives, engaged in the theologically sanctioned murder of atheists, pagans, and heretics.

The biblical scholars and apologists will insist "Thou shalt not kill" was mistranslated and should be "Thou shalt not commit murder". (Certainly, Moses had no compunction about killing folks.) But even with the correct translation, the many nuances of killing and murder are not addressed.

Discussion on the Concept of God

Benjamin Franklin wrote one of the most interesting essays on the matter of god. It is titled *A Dissertation On Liberty and Necessity, Pleasure and Pain.* Franklin wrote, "The great uncertainty I found in metaphysical reasoning disgusted me, and I quitted that kind of reading and study for others more satisfactory." In his view, theology and morality were divorced and he viewed social problems as problems to be solved by man, not god. Franklin started his essay on religion with two premises:

> There is said to be a First Mover, who is called God, maker of the Universe. He is said to be all wise, all good, and all-powerful. These two Propositions being allow'd and asserted by People of almost every Sect and Opinion; I have here suppos'd them granted, and laid them down as the foundation of my Argument. What follows then, being a Chain of Consequences truly drawn from them, will stand or fall as they are true or false.

Starting from these premises, Franklin listed some of the glaring contradictions that are noted in this chapter. Franklin wrote the essay in response to a friend's question and never meant it to be published. Thus his conclusion:

> I am sensible that the doctrine here Advanc'd, if it were to be publish'd, would meet with but an indifferent reception. Mankind naturally and generally love to be flattered....But, (to use a Piece of "Common sense")

our "Geese" are but "Geese" tho'
we may think em Swans; and Truth
will be Truth tho' it sometimes
prove mortifying and distasteful.

Explanations of the Weaknesses of the Definitions of God

Since the definitions of god are so full of holes, various attempts have been made to cover them up.

First, the existence of evil and the troubling, inexplicable, and horrible events in human history call into question the existence of a loving god. They are explained by saying that man has limited knowledge and thus is not smart enough to understand a perfect god. It is claimed that god works in mysterious ways or that man cannot understand the mystery of god. But in the next breath you are told exactly what god is doing and thinking.

Second, questions about the existence of god are stifled by means of implicit or explicit threats. Atheists have been killed for their beliefs. To this day, atheism is a dirty word. Boy Scouts, a wag said, would welcome a god-fearing cannibal into their ranks but wouldn't tolerate a principled atheist. Even believers in god were burned at the stake because their beliefs did not conform to the prevalent religious doctrine.

Third, an evil rival in the name of satan is introduced. While god is good, satan is evil. Anything that goes wrong can be attributed to satan and everything that is right attributed to god. On the other hand, if something goes wrong that cannot be blamed on satan, then it can be explained away by, "god works in mysterious ways." The saying that god works in mysterious ways means that we cannot determine whether god or satan is responsible for the horrible events in history.

Fourth, the concepts of heaven and hell are created as a reward and punishment system. People are divided into two groups: them and us. The believers in the right god go to heaven; all others go to hell for eternity.

Fifth, the concept of sin comes forth. This concept takes the responsibility for the presence of evil away from god and puts it elsewhere. Satan, of course, is a natural one to take over the responsibility for evil. But the brunt of the burden for mankind is borne by Adam and Eve, especially Eve. Poor Eve was hoodwinked by the sly satan, disobeyed god, and led all humanity into a world of sin for evermore.

Conclusion

The concept of god is a human invention. That is why we have so many religions, mythologies, and systems of belief. That is why the concept of god is so contradictory and illogical. Religions and mythologies simply differ in their time frames – old religions are mythologies – current mythologies are religions. Mainstream religions are sacred; unusual religions are cults.

It seems that there has always been a psychological need for belief in god and afterlife. The Egyptians and Chinese, for example, buried their dead and left valuables in their tombs for the afterlife. Likewise, the concepts of god, satan, evil, heaven, hell, the Garden of Eden, and Adam and Eve, make a nice and reasonably satisfying story for many. But it doesn't mean we should not question the concept of god and peel off the layers of superstition surrounding it.

Questions about God

Origin of god: When we consider the concept of an all-powerful, all-knowing, righteous, perfect being, we should ask, "Where did god come from? Did god create itself? Was there another creator?" Clearly these are questions that have no answers. However, it is not reasonable to believe that something can create itself.

God and the presence of evil: The existence and prevalence of evil, in the face of an all-knowing, all-powerful god is an issue that will not go away. If god is all-powerful but chooses not to destroy evil, then it is not all-good. If god is all-good but is unable to destroy evil, then it is not all-powerful. The theological mythology places the blame on Adam and Eve. We contend that it is simply wrong to place the blame on the least powerful members of the cast of characters—Adam and Eve did not have the knowledge and the awareness of evil nor did they have the skills to fight it. God was the only one who knew what was going on. It should have taken steps to thwart satan. When attempts to deal with satan's cunning failed, the responsibility rested with the most powerful being at the scene—that was god, not Adam and Eve.

According to prevalent theology, satan was god's creation. Satan was an angel. God endowed satan with supernatural powers. When god and satan had a falling out, god kicked satan out of heaven and ever since, satan has been causing problems not only for humanity but also for god. If god is the creator of everything, then god is the creator of evil.

The story of creation is just that – a story. The basic issue when it comes to human affairs is that dealing with satan is god's responsibility—not man's. Satan is more powerful than human beings because god gave satan powers that were denied to human beings. God, however, is more powerful than satan. It is god, therefore, who should do something about satan's mischief—e.g., take away satan's powers or uncreate him. If we believe the clergy, the devil has a bigger fiefdom than god. The clergy claim that only a select few, namely the clergy's followers, will be in heaven, the domain of god, while all the rest of the people will go to hell, the domain of satan. While satan may be god's creation and responsibility, certainly man's evil is man's responsibility.

Humans, unfortunately, are caught in this mythology of the struggle between god and satan. Humans are supposed to be helping god in this fight but with no clear guidelines. Some preachers maintain that faith in god is the only way to get to heaven and that doing good deeds on earth will not get you there. In their view, doing good deeds instead of being faithful to god is satan's clever ploy. The distinction between doing good deeds and being faithful to god is confusing as well as unfair. This is a means of twisting anything anyone thinks or does into satan's ploy, except for worshipping their god. Further, such beliefs discourage people from being helpful to others.

God and the age of science: We are in an age of reason and magnificent scientific, technical, and medical advances. None of the writers of the scriptures knew about the world as we do today. They did not know that the earth moved around the sun; they did not know about galaxies, black holes, and the expansion of the universe; they did not know that one day man would set foot on the moon and send rockets to other planets. In the light of all that has transpired, it is unreasonable to give unquestioned allegiance to scriptures written thousands of years ago. Neither should we allow preachers and theologians to get away with the pretension that they speak for god. Though many may know more about religion than you or I, none know more about god. Don't belittle yourself in the presence of the experts on religion – they are not experts on god.

A consequence of the age of reason is the reliance on skepticism and the scientific method. We now understand the importance of subjecting new medical devices and drugs to rigorous tests before distributing them widely to the general population. In that sense, we should also subject prayers to rigorous analysis. For example, can man get god to change its mind by praying? Can we reliably document that god changes its mind and gives the faithful whatever he or she is asking for? For example, one of the common themes in prayers is for universal peace. Is there peace in the world today? Many faithful believe prayer cures diseases. How true is it? What is the dosage of prayer – one prayer a day, one a week, five times a day? Or is the prayer's effectiveness dependent on the number of people engaged in it? If, for instance, a million people pray for world peace, are we more likely to get it?

In the case of medicines and medical devices, we have reasonable tests to evaluate the results. We should subject the efficacy of prayers to similar tests rather than depending upon the words of preachers. Prayer may have a second order effect on patients, that is, all things being equal a person who prays may have a slight edge. On the other hand, a cheerful person with a positive attitude towards life may have a similar or greater edge. For certain, the person with an upbeat positive attitude has an advantage over the depressed person who begs to god for help. It is foolish to depend on prayer for a cure of cancer or infection. Prayer doesn't cure cleft palates or repair damaged hearts. Begging is not praying, but praying is begging.

The issue of prayer has another dimension. Recall our analogy of the small town mayor. If god is willing to listen to the prayers of the faithful, where is the rule of law? Rapists and murderers who pray and say they believe as the clergy instruct, go to heaven while good people who don't believe will be sentenced to hell. It isn't logical or fair.

It may well be that prayer is a harmless fantasy, but it may also be used to manipulate people. If god responds to prayers, it means that god is capricious and is no longer just and fair to all people. If god doesn't answer prayers, it may well be because it doesn't have the power to grant the prayers. In any case, an all-knowing god does not need to depend on prayers to figure out what is going on in the world.

God and catch-22: God's capriciousness and tendency to punish in an arbitrary fashion, puts humans in a catch-22 situation. You are damned if you do and damned if you don't. Man is, in this view, sinful because he disobeyed god's will. St. Augustine, on the other hand, asserted that man was led to sin by a blindness, which god inflicts upon him. Now that's a catch-22 for you. God's punishment made us sinful, but god will punish us for eternity because we are sinful.

The concept of god is ambiguous: The concept of god is ambiguous and unrealistic because it is man's imperfect creation. Horace Kephart, in *Our Southern Highlanders,* wrote, "It is only a town-dreamed allegory that represents Nature as a fond mother suckling her young upon her breast. Those who have lived literally close to wild nature know her for a tyrant, from whom nothing can be wrung without toil and the risk of death." Even those living in an urban setting see Nature in that same light, with no mercy or pity for any living creature. The first lesson of a worthwhile life must be responsibility and self-reliance.

Look at the multitudes of religions, the large number of names for god, and the many descriptions of god's powers and actions. Unfortunately, there is no way to determine which version of god is true because god itself is silent on this matter. But logic tells us that an all-knowing, all-powerful being must be held responsible and accountable for everything.

Perhaps you will know you have met god when you shake hands with someone you cannot see, hear, smell, feel, or touch. In reality, people create their own individual god that satisfies their intellectual and emotional needs. Some call their god Love, Nature, Force, Energy, Spirit, or First Cause. Others become Deists and believe that god created the cosmos and then retired from active duty, leaving man to forage for himself. Most people realize they must depend upon themselves and their fellow man.

Human beings have always created their own supernatural beings. Their demons, witches, sorcerers, spirits, angels, devils, gods, and goddesses were all created out of fear, desperation, hope, and lack of knowledge.

In one of the *Peanuts* comic strips, Charlie says to Snoopy, "I find it strange that the golfing Gods have never allowed you to make a hole in one.... I wonder what that means." Snoopy replies, "It means we need some new golfing Gods."

If your god does not do what you want, do as Snoopy does, create a new one.

15

In the end, we should require any god to be as good as man. The oft-repeated epitaph applies here:

> *Here lie I, Martin Elginbrod;*
> *Have mercy on my soul,*
> *Lord God,*
> *As I would do, were I*
> *Lord God,*
> *And ye were Martin Elginbrod.*

Religion is regarded by the common people as true, by the wise as false, and by rulers as useful.

Seneca the Younger

THE WORD OF GOD

Religions such as Christianity, Islam, and Judaism claim that their scriptures are the word of god. Christianity, for instance, claims that god revealed the Bible to the authors and that it is the word of god. Mormons claim that an angel inscribed the word of god on golden tablets, which Joseph Smith and his cronies dug up, but no one else has ever seen. Now over eleven million people profess to believe that. Jews claim that god gave the Ten Commandments to Moses. Muhammad, Jesus, and many others have claimed that they received the word of god directly from god itself or through angels.

The word of god, by definition, is the truth. Therefore, truths conveyed through the scriptures are eternal and unchangeable. Some fundamentalists believe that every word in the Bible is literally true. Many Christians ardently believe that one does not need any other book but the Bible to understand truth and morality.

The followers of religions such as Christianity and Islam believe that they have a mandate to spread the word of god around the world. Christians spend enormous resources through missionary and evangelical activities to spread the word of god. Religions have frequently chosen the sword and forced conversions to spread that word.

It is said that god's words are awe-inspiring and demand unquestioned obedience. God's words, it is claimed, are the basis of society, law, and justice. Without the word of god, by extension, there will be chaos, lawlessness, and injustice. Also the word of god shows the way to salvation and heaven.

Problems with the word of god: God was not consistent in revealing its word. It gave one version to Jews, one to the followers of Jesus, and yet another version to Muhammad. None of these versions agree with the words it gave to the Greeks, Hindus, and Buddhists. God's revelations are like a rich uncle that promises to his nieces and nephews that each one alone will inherit his estate upon his death. Every religion claims that it alone is the repository of truth. Not surprisingly, as in the case of potential inheritors of a rich uncle's estate, this concept has caused a great amount of conflict between the followers of the various religions.

But the problem with god's words does not end there. Among Christians, for instance, there are many versions of the Bible as well as many translations and interpretations. Christians first split into Roman Catholic and Eastern Orthodox Churches. Protestants then broke off from the Roman Catholic Church. Protestants then divided into a multitude of denominations such as Baptist, Mormon, Methodist, Episcopalian, and so on and on. All these schisms and breakups cite the word of god for support. (Someone recently counted 9900 religions in the world today.) It should be noted that every new religion was created by someone who was dissatisfied with the old one. A new doctrine first begins as a cult; when it gains a significant following, it becomes a religion.

There are many ambiguities in the word of god. Theologians endlessly discuss the nuances of god's words. Some interpretations are considered authoritative while others are considered heretical. In the past, some heretics were swiftly dispatched for their contrarian beliefs. In the Christian tradition, for instance, there is a long-standing difference of opinion as to whether good works in this world are sufficient to send someone to heaven or faith alone is the basis for entering heaven. Both points of view derive their support from the same Bible, the same word of god.

The word of god contains contradictory messages. Many religions claim to be peaceful and yet they harbor threats to nonbelievers. Jesus himself demonstrates this dichotomy. He says, "But love ye your enemies, and do good, and lend, hoping for nothing again; and your reward shall be great, and ye shall be the children of the Highest: for he is kind unto the unthankful and to the evil." *(Luke 6: 35)*. On the other hand, Jesus continued to castigate people who did not believe that he was the Messiah. He created us *vs.* them categories.

He called believers people of god and those who did not believe in him as people not of god, when he said, "He that is of God heareth God's words; ye therefore hear them not, because ye are not of God." *(John 8:47)*.

The words of god are ambiguous in other ways. Readers of every persuasion can derive support from them. Both the supporters and opponents of slavery in the United States claimed theological support from the Bible although the Biblical authors took slavery for granted and did not have much to say about the kind of slavery that was practiced in the United States or the Roman Empire. The supporters and opponents of capital punishment can both find justification in the Bible for their views.

God's words are considered parables or metaphors by most, rather than literal truths. On the other hand, there are people who swear by the Bible and say that every word therein should be read literally, not metaphorically.

Many of the words of god were revealed hundreds or thousands of years ago. Since then human societies have gone through breathtaking changes through social, political, industrial, trade, scientific, and technical advances. Writers of scriptures had no clue that one-day human beings would land on the moon and send artificial satellites to other planets. The Bible dwells on Egypt and the Roman Empire. Those empires no longer exist. Jews, the chosen people of god, have gone through upheavals and holocausts during the intervening centuries, which prompted a Jewish wag to pray, "Lord, please choose someone else for a change."

All these differences cause conflicts between religions, sects, and denominations. Religious conflicts, even in the twenty-first century, are major threats to world peace.

Conclusion: God's words, despite the claims of religions, are ambiguous and equivocal. God's chosen methods of spreading his word, through revelation, divine inspiration, and so on, are rife with problems because everyone has a different interpretation of those words and people tend to hear what they want to hear. Certainly, no god would send its word by way of an impressionable, neurotic, teenage girl.

The word of god is vague and poorly communicated. Rules laid out by god are easily flouted. Minor violations may bring on god's wrath while god allows clever people to discover and create loopholes. For instance, in Christianity one can be a wretch his entire life but can be guaranteed an entrée into heaven by confessing on the deathbed and accepting Jesus. Some proclaim themselves born again and are sure they will go to heaven, while all others who either have never heard of the born-again concept or are incredulous of such a claim, will be destined for hell.

Thomas Paine had this to say about the Bible:

> Whenever we read the obscene stories, the voluptuous debaucheries, the cruel and torturous

executions, the unrelenting vindictiveness with which more than half the Bible is filled, it would be more consistent that we called it the word of a demon than the word of God. It has served to corrupt and brutalize mankind.

The word of god is often a cruel word. The word seems to emphasize god's wrath – lightning, famines, tornadoes, earthquakes, fires, diseases, and floods – as a way of keeping people in line and keeping them obedient and faithful. St. Thomas Aquinas revealed Christianity at its worst when he said, "The blessed in heaven will walk to the battlements and look down with delight in the justice of God being properly carried out in hell." Apparently heaven and hell are close together.

Christ frequently threatened people with hell; "Ye serpents, ye generation of vipers, how can ye escape the damnation of hell." *(Matthew 23: 33)*. Obviously, Jesus believed in hell, and he threatened eternal damnation for those who disagreed with him.

There are many who are convinced the Ten Commandments are the direct word of god. However, the commandments may be simply viewed as the beginnings of a human societal organization and, specifically, the organization of Jewish society. They are social, moral, and religious codes to live by. Probably, Moses claimed god's authorship of these commands because of the awe and unquestioned obedience such a claim entailed. However, these commands were not and are not unique to Jewish society. All societies have similar codes of social behavior that go back hundreds of years. Buddha preached the philosophy of nonviolence over twenty five hundred years ago. Likewise, Egyptian society was functioning for thousands of years before the birth of Jesus and it must have had a dependable social code for it to survive as long as it did. The commandments never to steal, commit murder, covet neighbor's goods, commit adultery, or give false testimony, are basic rules necessary to survive in any group.

In reality, the word of god is the word of man. Man wrote the scriptures and claimed god's authorship in order to obtain legitimacy and obedience. One should remember that even now, literacy is low in many societies and not everyone who can read and write likes to write. Writing is a hard task. Thousands of years ago, the absolute number and percentage of people who could read and write was very small. It was easy to claim that the written word was the word of god and to further claim that those words were inspired or revealed by god.

It is time for people to acknowledge that the words of god are really the words of man. God's words as related by man, like any other human endeavor, are prone to error and can stand careful scrutiny and revision without a fear of going to hell. In the end, man's first and foremost commandment should be:

YOU ARE RESPONSIBLE FOR ALL OF YOUR ACTIONS.

If you look carefully, this statement summarizes the Ten Commandments.

Bertrand Russell was asked at his ninetieth birthday party, "What if when you die you find yourself facing God, what will you say?"

Russell replied, "I should say, 'God, you gave us insufficient evidence'."

There is nothing more frightening than active ignorance.

Goethe

Doing the Lord's Work

One frequently hears that people are called to do god's work. What is god's work? The phrase "god's work" is used to denote a number of ideas and activities. They include entering the ministry/ priesthood in order to spread the word of god; preaching faith in god; helping the poor and the sick by setting up hospitals; establishing schools and colleges to improve literacy; and setting up charitable organizations to serve the poor and the needy.

The notion of doing the Lord's work has benefited society in many respects. Religion-sponsored hospitals treated the sick and provided medical care. Individuals such as Mother Teresa in India took their calling seriously and helped those who were ignored by the rest of society. On the educational level, a large number of American colleges and universities, many of which are world famous, were started by religious denominations. The Catholic Church has been active at all levels of education and strives to provide quality education along with religious and moral indoctrination to its faithful. In the field of charitable activities, religious bodies have been at the forefront in serving society. Religious organizations have provided needed services to the poor. Jewish organizations, in addition to serving the poor, have contributed to the national life of the arts. Members of many denominations rushed to New York to assist people in the wake of the September 11, 2001 terrorist attack.

But doing god's work has many negative consequences. Doing god's work and spreading god's word went hand in hand with the colonization and suppression of colonized people. Once people are identified as pagans, barbarians, or infidels, it is easy to demonize, dehumanize, and destroy them. For some, doing god's work means killing an infidel, witch, or any rival of their god. Doing god's work can mean silencing any objective thought or discussion of god. History is replete with the stories of horrors inflicted on infidels and conquered people by religious believers. The result of all this horror was genocide and the destruction of many civilizations, cultures, and languages. Another consequence, ironically, was the introduction of vices such as alcoholism as well as the introduction of new diseases such as small pox and syphilis to Native Americans.

There are other aspects of doing god's work. What exactly is god's work? God by definition is omnipotent and omniscient. It created the universe. If such is the case, why does god need anyone's help? Why doesn't god do its own work? Since god created the cosmos, we cannot determine what its job is or what its wishes are. Why are we, with our limited abilities, resources, and short life spans called upon to help an all-powerful, all-knowing, eternal being? As a parent is responsible for its offspring, so too is a god who created the cosmos and mankind, responsible for its creations. God seems to be like some parents who create their children, then ignore them or even mistreat them. If there is such a god, it is not doing a credible job.

Doing god's work makes as much sense as giving a penny to a rich man. God does not and should not need man to do its work. The iron rule should be evoked here. "Do not do for others what they won't take the time or effort to do for themselves." An all-powerful god is fully capable of doing for itself and if it wants something done right, it had better do it itself.

How does one know god's will? God doesn't speak to us in plain language or in such a way that everybody the world over can understand it. We don't know if it is confused or if we are confused since we hear different messages coming from the same god. We are told that god doesn't want you to fly on the Sabbath; god doesn't want you to transact business on the Sabbath; god doesn't want you to shop on the Sabbath; god wants its ambiguous, much disobeyed, and ignored commandments posted in all of the schools and courthouses; god wants to be praised constantly; god wants you to kill an infidel or a physician who does abortions, and so on and on. One could write a book on all of god's wants and wishes – they are all over the place and often contradict themselves. Supposedly, it is harder for rich people to go to heaven but god blesses its faithful with riches. Many of god's desires are rather silly and superfluous in the context of our global village. God hasn't even been clear on which day the Sabbath is to be observed – some observe on Saturday and others on Sunday. One person's Sabbath is another's workday. Round the clock, round the week, and round the year, somebody some place is working, shopping, flying, doing business, and fighting wars. Resting one day a week in an agrarian society makes sense, but we are no longer an agrarian society. Most of god's alleged wishes are not important enough for man to waste his time on, let alone be a serious concern for a god. Fortunately or unfortunately, most people practice "cafeteria religion" – they simply pick and choose what they want out of their creeds and dogmas.

The religious experts who are telling you what god wants should be told in no uncertain terms, "Have god talk to me." An all-knowing, all-powerful being can and will get whatever it wants. An all-powerful being will obtain happiness if that is what it desires, it will not depend upon fallible man. We do not need the clergy to tell us what god wants.

Some entrepreneur should create a board game called *Let's Play God.* It would have squares with all of the challenges of life, good and bad. After throwing the dice and advancing to one of the squares, one draws a card telling what god desires. God may instruct you to pray more; turn the other cheek; give away all of your material assets; become a missionary and convert the pagans; burn the heretics at the stake; feed the hungry; even crash a plane into the World Trade Center. The game would be a good exercise revealing god's unpredictability. It would also show god's mysterious ways. Finally, it would reveal how dependent we are upon fate and just plain dumb luck.

Put yourself in god's shoes. What would you do if you had unlimited power and knew everything? Wouldn't you stop the senseless wars? Wouldn't you stop the planes from flying into World Trade Center? Wouldn't you stop the suffering from hurricanes, floods, and other natural disasters? Wouldn't you stop drunk drivers from killing innocent people? We bet that ninety-nine percent of the population would be more kind and caring than the present god.

We should recognize a couple of things when we are talking about doing god's work. Many of those who are engaged in doing god's work are not completely selfless. On the contrary, they are often after our money and labor. Doing god's work benefits them immensely. They get to eat better, live better, lord over us, judge us, and demand money and obedience from us. You don't often see thin and emaciated preachers. You may notice that preachers often are the alpha males in our society.

One should also remember that altruism has always existed among human beings as well as in other species of the animal kingdom. If you look at your own community you will see a number of people who work as teachers, social workers, and organizers and employees of nonprofit organizations. Many of them are volunteers or work for low wages, but all are dedicated to improving the lives of the people around them. These dedicated women and men do not enjoy the visibility and prestige of preachers who proclaim that they are engaged in doing god's work.

Finally, being charitable and kind to your fellow man comes naturally to some people. Helping each other guarantees human survival. It is enlightened self-interest. Man was kind, charitable, and helpful long before a monotheistic god came into the picture. In modern times, we can say that being considerate, charitable, and kind to our fellow man is humanism at its best.

I shall pass through this world but once. If, therefore, there be any kindness I can show, or any good thing I can do, let me do it now; let me not defer it or neglect it, for I shall not pass this way again.

Etienne de Grellet

EVANGELISM

Evangelism, in its broader sense of spreading one's faith and converting people of other faiths, often against heavy odds, is not a new phenomenon. Buddhism, Christianity, and Islam have been the three major religions to send missionaries to convert others. The followers of Buddha, for example, starting from India, spread their faith over a large geographic area including Sri Lanka, China, and Japan. But in modern times, evangelism primarily represents Christian and Muslim activity with the purpose of spreading the "good news" and seeking converts to their faith. Christians derive their mandate for evangelism from Jesus who commissioned his followers to go out into the world and preach the good news. They were to baptize and convert as they went. *(Matthew 28: 18-20)* Jesus' earliest missionaries were his twelve disciples.

Evangelism represents Christians' genuine belief that they are engaged in the process of saving souls. Converting nonbelievers to the Christian faith will ensure that the souls of the converts, along with those of the rest of the believers, will go to heaven after their death. Mormons, Baptists, and many other Christian churches routinely send their missionaries to all corners of the globe, seeking converts. Nonbelievers are encouraged and enticed to convert to Christianity by various means. For instance, missionaries are expected to serve as moral role models for the nonbeliever and exhibit compassion, love, and faith. Other means include assisting the nonbelievers by distributing food, building churches, and helping them in times of crisis such as wars, famines, and catastrophes. Others send religious information and pamphlets to the unbelievers of their faith. Thomas Jefferson in 1816 wrote to a Mrs. H. Harrison Smith on this subject:

> I never told my own religion nor scrutinized that of another. I never attempted to make a convert, nor wished to change another's creed. I am satisfied that yours must be an excellent religion to have produced a life of such exemplary virtue and correctness. For it is in our lives, not from our words, that our religion must be judged.

But there is a dark side to evangelism. Many evangelists are zealots who are driven to get others to believe as they do. Some will do whatever is necessary to convince others to their way of thinking. Zealots are coercive, manipulative, and often cruel. They pretend to be friends and interested in you but are primarily interested in claiming you as their success story—they are like con men or like people who keep count of their sexual conquests. Evangelists believe that they rack up points with god for every convert they make. Evangelists, by converting others to their way of thinking, reinforce their own beliefs.

The zealotry of the evangelicals means that there is a dogmatism and rigidity in their thinking. They are fearful of new ideas, especially those that seem to contradict or undermine their beliefs. John Adams, according to David McCullough's carefully researched biography of our second president, was concerned with this issue as he wrestled to choose between ministry and law. Adams, a Unitarian, finally decided against the ministry saying, "I saw such a spirit of dogmatism and bigotry in clergy or laity, that if I should be a priest I must take my side and pronounce as positively as any of them, or never get a parish, or getting it must soon leave it."

Under the delusion that they are working for god, evangelists, fundamentalists, and fanatics have in the past and continue to do evil in the name of god. The Inquisition, the Holy Crusades, and the burning of witches have been well documented. While some evangelists are sincere, political leaders use their teachings to motivate others to murder, kill, and hate. John Hemming in *The Conquest of the Incas* wrote that the Indians of Peru were to be robbed, enslaved, and killed if they did not accept Christianity. The Spaniards maintained that the results would be the fault of those who did not accept Christ, not theirs. They had an obligation to Christianize the natives. Evangelists still feel that same obligation today.

Empathy, the placing of oneself in another's position, is a commendable human trait. It makes one kinder, more tolerant, and more humane – even more generous. Man seems to have an inborn desire to help others who are suffering. Those with Bible and god in hand have another motive that cheapens and decreases empathy. Although these zealots may honestly believe they are saving the recipient from the wrath of a god who would otherwise send them to hell, that belief subtracts from both kindness and empathy. Those who give of themselves and their worldly goods without that motive are more truly charitable.

Thomas Jefferson had misgivings about missionary activity and said, "I do not know that it is a duty to disturb by missionaries the religion and peace of other countries." Mark Twain, with tongue-in-cheek, expressed his concern for the native Hawaiians. He felt sorrow for them because before the missionaries arrived they died without knowing about hell. We can be thankful that missionaries are "spreading the word" and converting all of those pagans and heathens into god-fearing citizens.

Evangelists employ fear in spreading the word of god. Pat Robertson recently said, "The Lord is getting ready to shake this nation. We have not yet seen his judgment on

America...This thing that happened in New York was child's play compared to what's going to happen." Aren't we fortunate that we have people like Pat who not only know what god wants, but what it has done in the past and what its future plans are?

The belief that man has a soul that will separate from the body and is capable of an eternity of happiness or damnation allows the fanatics to justify any means of cruelty to be certain that one is saved from god's cruelty. After all, what are a few years in this life compared with eternity? The belief that man can live forever in heaven if he believes a certain way, allows evil under the guise of caring and love.

The evangelist believes that he has a special relationship with god and wants you to believe that he knows exactly how you can get into heaven. He will even ask god to forgive the murderer, rapist, or felon who is facing death. To believe that heaven is available to folks who are not fit to live in human society stretches one's credulity. How any self-respecting god would forgive and let those folks into heaven taxes logic.

Religions are built upon myths, rituals, festivals, and beliefs but in the end they are based on the carrot of heaven and the stick of hell. The most notorious of these hells is the one dreamed up by Dante. Dante's hell is the result of a deranged imagination. If you listen to the radio and television preachers or to those who spew out venom on the street corners, you will note that they use Dante's imagery to frighten people into conversion. Billy Graham, our country's most noted and beloved evangelist built his early ministry through his fiery sermons, but he has mellowed with age. He said that he used to think of hell as Dante's hell. Now, he interprets hell as a separation from god. That is a major difference. Billy Graham may have given up on Dante's hell, but you can be sure the other fiery preachers will not. Religions and denominations must keep Dante's hell to survive and grow. It is important for religion to have fear to keep up attendance and to keep donations coming in.

There is another aspect to evangelism. As it is practiced, it is masculine, full of testosterone and warlike aggressiveness. In fact, many evangelicals see themselves as soldiers. Their god is equally masculine. Evangelists are dogmatic, positive, and loud. As Ambrose Bierce noted, "Positive is mistaken at the top of one's voice." It takes a stern, masculine, demanding god to get you to church every Sabbath and to talk you out of ten percent of your income.

This author vividly remembers one night long ago when his mother told him and his brothers to be quiet and go to sleep. When they didn't, she came up the stairs with a flimsy yardstick and proceeded to spank them. The yardstick broke into pieces and the author, his brothers, and their mother all burst out laughing. Boy, what a punishment it was! The truth is that it is hard for us to imagine our mothers sentencing us to hell. When we recall our childhood, it is not our moms' stern punishment that comes to our minds but the smells of cooking, food, nourishment, laughter, and happiness as we snuggle with our mother. Despite all of the evangelicals' preaching, it is hard to feel the same warmth from an aggressive, judgmental, masculine god.

In our family we have a rule for arguments, disagreements, and discussions. We call it "Calling the question". After all sides have been presented and the participants are simply repeating their arguments, anyone can call the question. That call ends the discussion until further information is available or until you look up the answer. The discussion will be resumed only when participants can present new information or proof. Now is the time to call the question on the following points of discussion:

■ There is a supernatural being called God, Allah, Yahweh, Zeus, or Apollo who is in control of the universe and actively running it *vs.* There is no such being.

■ My god is better than your god *vs.* No, it isn't, my god is better than your god.

■ My religion, church, or sect has all the right answers *vs.* No, yours doesn't, mine does.

■ There is a life after death, a heaven and a hell *vs.* No, there is no life after death, no heaven, and no hell.

Those basic beliefs and disbeliefs are the differences between believers and between believers and nonbelievers. They have been argued, discussed, and fought over for centuries. It is time to call the question. Until further proof is available, it is futile to continue the discussion. If we could stop those arguments, then the fights, killings, and wars over those basic differences, which cannot be proven one way or another with our present knowledge, would be greatly diminished. Buddha advised his followers not to waste their time and energy speculating about god, as it is impossible to determine if it exists. Buddha further advised his followers to avoid all religious creeds and dogmas when seeking guidance. Until we have more information concerning god, we should "call the question".

Religious beliefs should be personal and private. For the sake of humanity, organized religions must not be allowed to preach their hatred of others.

Certainty generally is illusion, and repose is not the destiny of man.
Oliver Wendell Holmes, Jr.

IMMORTALITY

Man has always had difficulty accepting death and in believing in his own nonexistence after death. He can comprehend and accept nonexistence before he was born but he cannot accept it after he experiences life. Since man does not want to accept his own demise, he seeks the solace of religion, which allows him to believe he will live forever. Men and women have been in awe of life and death since their first awareness.

Not everybody believes that they bodily go to heaven, although some do and they believe that Jesus is coming to gather their rotting bodies or ashes, resurrect them, and all will march to their glory in heaven. The belief that cremation was wrong was based on the thought that one would have a harder time getting to heaven from their ashes than from their decomposed body. One must remember, only those who do as the priest, preacher, rabbi, or mullah says will be eligible for the trip. Religions build upon the desire for immortality, everlasting life in heaven, and the fear of eternal damnation in hell.

In one sense you do not need to believe in an all-knowing, all-powerful being to believe in immortality. On the other hand, you need a scorekeeper to separate those going to the different places. Even the believers in reincarnation must have someone or something deciding whether a person's next life will be as a bug or a Buddha. You can visualize massive computer banks storing and retrieving data on each and every one of us. Oh! How our governments would love to have that ability.

There is a comforting side to the belief in immortality. It comforts many people to believe that their loved ones are enjoying a happy afterlife. It may allow them to grieve less if they believe there is a humane reason for early death, whether by accident or disease. It allows them to accept the unpredictability and the unfairness of life. It allows them to believe that their deceased loved one is alive and happy with god and the angels.

On the other hand, the concept of heaven allows people to justify death, illness, and the unfairness of life. For instance, some people comfort themselves when a loved one is killed by a drunk driver by saying that the loved one is free of pain and suffering and is now residing with the Lord. It sounds like the drunk has been an instrument of the Lord and allowed a good person to die and go to heaven sooner than usual. Just think, most people have to wait for old age to enjoy heaven but thanks to the drunk, this innocent person has gone to heaven early. The whole rationale sounds like we should reward drunks and murderers.

We must acknowledge that we do not know what will happen to us after we die. We know that we did not exist before our parents' ovum and sperm united. We also know that our body, including our brain that is responsible for all thoughts, ideas, feelings, and beliefs, deteriorates and rots after death. As a result of that knowledge most cannot logically conclude that humans will continue to exist in any thinking, feeling form after death. The belief in immortality seems a farfetched wish.

The belief in immortality originated when man and his world were the center of the universe and god was alleged to have created man in his own image. Man thought of himself as special and unique in the universe and therefore had special privileges. Of course males who were in control of such things at that time considered themselves even more special and privileged than females.

Thanks to Charles Darwin, we now know that we share our evolution with the animal and plant life around us. We share our genes with other life forms. Our bodies are composed of chemicals, and chemical and biological knowledge continues to reveal that we are subject to the same chemical and biological rules that govern every other life form. We share genes not only with apes but also with insects and bacteria. We don't believe that insects will go to heaven after they die. What is so special about us? The believers in immortality cannot comprehend or live with the idea that man is a part of the vast global food chain and that the bugs and insects will ultimately enjoy us. We may not want to accept the fact that we are part of the food chain, but that does not alter the truth of it.

Believe as you will in immortality; just don't pay too much for your ticket to heaven.

The average man, who does not know what to do with this life, wants another one which shall last forever.

Anatole France

God is Ignorance

Man has always created his gods and goddesses out of hope, fear, and ignorance. When faced with difficult circumstances, man has always invoked the help of unseen gods and prayed for deliverance from harm. It is satisfying to hope for a heaven after one's death to compensate for life's difficulties; it is satisfying to hope for eternal damnation for one's powerful and ruthless enemies. For eons, man has faced problems that he did not understand and did not know how to explain. Examples of these are earthquakes, cyclones, tornadoes, lightning, floods, droughts, hurricanes, diseases, fires, wars, and death. The more unknowns, the more man calls on gods for explanations. Since no explanations of these natural events were available, it was easy to believe that god had something to do with them. These life's problems were thought to be the result of one god or another being unhappy with mankind. Man could not even explain the pleasant things in his life such as the beauty of flowers, trees, mountains, trickling springs, and valleys. Again, god came to the rescue. It is all god's doing. Everything is god's handiwork. Since many things cannot be explained with the existing knowledge, it is necessary to fall back on the explanation that god is mysterious. But mystery is ignorance; mystery is simply the lack of knowledge.

As we look back in history, we see many things that were initially attributed to god but are no longer. During the 80's when AIDS struck the United States and the rest of the world, scientists like everyone else, were baffled by the disease; they did not know what caused AIDS and they had no clue as to how to cure it. Into this breach entered the religious establishment claiming that AIDS was god's way of punishing homosexual men who were engaged in unnatural sexual acts. Later, medical researchers identified the cause of the disease and, however imperfectly, found a way to control it. We now know that AIDS not only attacks homosexual men but also women, heterosexual men, innocent people who received transfusions of tainted blood, monogamous individuals who were unfortunate enough to come into contact with the AIDS virus, and innocent babies. With the gaining of knowledge about AIDS, we seldom hear the ravings of preachers who maintain that an angry god sent AIDS to punish homosexual behavior. One can only wonder what god has in mind with SARS.

AIDS is but one example. We now know what causes earthquakes; we know which geographic areas are susceptible; we know how to build our houses, roads, and other structures to withstand earthquakes. We cannot predict specifically where and when they will strike, but now only idiots believe that earthquakes are the work of god.

We have, unlike the people who lived even a hundred years ago, better knowledge of weather patterns, when and where cyclones and hurricanes are likely to hit, and how much rain and snowfall we can expect. We now know that god did not cause droughts but rather they are due to unpredictable weather patterns. We may blame the Weather Channel if we don't like the weather but god is no longer in the picture for most people.

During the last two hundred years, we have learned more about viruses, bacteria, and how certain diseases are caused. We have learned more about how to prevent and control them. Many diseases that struck terror in the hearts of our ancestors and were thought to be the work of god are now but distant memories. If you look back in history, it was god that caused plagues, typhoid, sexually transmitted diseases, tuberculosis, pneumonia, as well as many other diseases. Today only the religious fanatics believe that. Now, when faced with these illnesses, we simply call our physician.

The brain is the most complicated and the least understood organ in the human body. There is much that is unknown about thoughts, ideas, dreams, feelings, emotions, and beliefs. Out of this lack of knowledge concerning the brain and its activities, a whole host of theories and concepts have been proposed. When we listen to the music of a great composer, see the great works of art, or read wonderful literary works, some admire them and attribute them to gifts from god. Our ignorance of the functioning of the brain leads us to believe in revelations from god, witchcraft, spirituality, intuition, ghosts, the supernatural, and a host of others. As the knowledge of the brain increases, most of these supernatural explanations will wither away. The words "mind" and "spirit" are ambiguous and in reality we have only thoughts that emanate from our perishable brain.

God grows smaller as man's knowledge increases. Science and intelligence decrease god's influence in law, politics, and life.

Despite our vastly increasing knowledge, we are still ignorant of many things. There are still many vexing philosophical questions for which we have no answers. Many questions trouble us such as the purpose of the universe, how and why our universe came into existence, the purpose of life, what happens after death, and so forth. Some of the questions are paradoxes; others are questions that are unknowable and unanswerable with our present knowledge. That lack of knowledge allows charlatans and religious people free rein.

God is a powerful tool. For centuries, god spoke only to priests who were the intermediaries between man and god. Thus, not only was god based upon ignorance but it was also a tool for powerful priests who used that ignorance to convince others to do their bidding. The hellfire and damnation of a charismatic preacher can make the most courageous man shake in his boots and obey the preacher's directives. However, it is not worth the time or effort to try to reason with the preacher who dogmatically exclaims, "God created man perfect at 9:00 AM on the 21st of October, 4004 BC." As Edmund Burke noted, you cannot reason a person out of a belief he was never reasoned into in the first place.

Fear of god is inculcated from childhood. Children, by nature, are curious and inquisitive. When told about god creating the universe and everything in it, children will respond with the question, "Who created god?" More often than not, their intellectual curiosity will be nipped in the bud. In response to their logical questions, they will get answers such as, "God works in mysterious ways" or, "Our simple minds just cannot understand God in all of his mystery and majesty." Even worse, they will hear, "Hush, hush, God does not like to be criticized and you will go to hell if you continue to question." Not only will their inquisitiveness be stifled, but also they will be indoctrinated and taught to be afraid of god. The children may never be able to think about god's actions and inactions again without fear and trepidation. Arthur Schopenhauer noted years ago, "There is no absurdity so palpable but that it may be implanted in the human head if you only begin to inculcate it before the age of five, by constantly repeating it with an air of great solemnity."

Over and over we see that our ignorance of the cause of the cosmos is used to justify a belief in god. As Sir William Osler noted, "The greater the ignorance the greater the dogmatism." Neither philosophy, theology, nor science can definitively answer the question of whom, why, or what created the universe. Physicists, chemists, astronomers, mathematicians, and other scientists are constantly expanding our knowledge of the cosmos. As knowledge of the cosmos increases, god is being pushed into a smaller and smaller corner of the universe.

Believers of god came up with the notion of intelligent design to account for our lack of knowledge – a direct descendent of the discredited creation theory. The supporters of intelligent design maintain that the universe is so wonderful, beautiful, complex, and orderly that there must be a conscious, thinking designer who obviously is god. Intelligent design is yet another name for our ignorance. If we don't know how a certain part of an organism works, we can quickly jump on the bandwagon and say, "See, the eyes are so beautiful and complex, they must be the result of the work of an intelligent designer." In reality, intelligent design is shorthand for "at this time, we don't know how it works or how it came about". The universe is not orderly and never has been. It is changing daily. It is constantly evolving. Even as we speak, drug-resistant bacteria are evolving somewhere. It is more reasonable to conclude that the cosmos, with its many deficiencies, was the result of unintelligent design rather than that of an intelligent design. Unintelligent design better describes the condition of the universe and the human race.

Anyone who would design a system where a seven-pound baby has to come out of a two inch hole has to be a sadist. Or, how about a one centimeter kidney stone lodged in a three millimeter ureter? Not to mention a worthless appendix that gets infected and requires surgery. (Maybe god is partial to general surgeons.) It should be obvious to all who are willing to look at the universe, its contents, and its randomness, that no intelligent being could be responsible for it. No matter what they teach the medical students at Loyola and Loma Linda medical schools, there is no way that the human body could have been created by an intelligent designer. If an intelligent designer is responsible for the universe and man, it has to be a malevolent one, not a benevolent one. If there was a struggle between satan and god – satan won.

If the cosmos must have a designer, we are again faced with the unanswerable question, "Who created the designer – a super designer?" Logic tells us that if everything must have a cause, there can be no first cause.

When believers are confronted with logical questions as to why god would allow or create the tragedies that befall humankind, they maintain that we humans are just not smart enough to understand god in its great wisdom. On the other hand, believers understand god perfectly when they hear god tell them to get on their knees and face Mecca and pray five times a day; or when it tells them to stand at the Wailing Wall and gyrate back and forth incessantly; or have your child confirmed; or to be born again by having holy water sprinkled on your head – better still, be totally immersed. Mark Twain was right, "It ain't what a man don't know what hurts him; it's what he knows that ain't true that does it."

Mortimer Adler in *How to Think About God* concludes that to believe in god was reasonable based on accepting the cosmology argument or the argument by design. However, he did not find it reasonable to believe in a personal god. As for immortality, Adler found no reason to believe in immortality, whether god existed or not. Finally he concluded that there was no reason to believe that god, who may or may not exist, cares about men and women or what happens to them.

In summary, it was not knowledge, logic, and reasoning that created gods, goddesses, and religions; it was hope, fear, and ignorance. Beliefs in religion have never been based on truth and knowledge but on mystery, myth, desire, fear, and forced or voluntary indoctrination. While many equate god to love, in reality, god is ignorance.

We should emulate Galileo and say, "I know it not" and then enjoy life. The admission of ignorance is the springboard for acquiring new knowledge.

Believers cannot prove that god exists, just as nonbelievers cannot prove that it does not. It really doesn't matter. It should be noted that it is up to believers to prove their premises, not up to nonbelievers to prove a negative.

The only thing that matters in life is whether you are moral, amoral, or immoral.

For ignorance is the mother of devotion, as all the world knows.

Robert Burton

A great deal of intelligence can be invested in ignorance when the need for illusion is deep.

Saul Bellow

FAITH

Faith, as the word is used in religion, is a belief in god and the veracity of sacred texts and doctrines. In Christianity, faith encompasses a belief in a monotheistic personal god, Jesus Christ as the Savior, the virgin birth, crucifixion, resurrection, and the truthfulness of the Bible. Each religion has a set of fundamental beliefs that form the core of their faith.

Religious faiths, beliefs, and convictions do not rest on logic or evidence. Faith is a belief in something that cannot be proved. No one can prove or disprove the existence of god. No one can prove or disprove that god is interested in having a personal relationship with each and every human being on the earth. One either believes it or doesn't. One need not be ashamed of having faith, but to believe in something that cannot be proven is nothing to brag about either. Walter Kaufman noted that, "Faith means intense, usually confident, belief that is not based on evidence sufficient to command assent from every reasonable person."

Religious faith is not the only faith we live with. We live our lives on faith, assumptions, and suppositions. When we leave our house and get into our car, we have faith that every one on the road will follow the traffic rules and regulations and that we will arrive home safely at the end of the day. We would be psychologically paralyzed if we did not have faith.

We must depend on faith because our knowledge is limited and our ignorance is vast. We cannot predict the future; consequently the decisions that pertain to the future depend upon faith, assumptions, and presumptions, along with a lot of limited knowledge. Knowledge by definition has been proven; faith has not.

The degree of certainty with faith, or any other belief, varies from unlikely to absolute. One's actions depend upon the certainty of one's beliefs. It is possible that someone somewhere believes that he or she can fly through the clouds unaided by any mechanical contraptions. With our knowledge, we know that this particular belief is impossible. Someone else may believe that he can drive at the speed of a hundred miles an hour without being ticketed by police; we know that it is unlikely but not impossible. There are other beliefs that we know are true. If we jump unaided from the second floor window, we know that we will land on the ground below and are likely to hurt ourselves because we don't know of a single example where someone has stayed suspended in the air. All beliefs are not equal.

In the case of most of our beliefs, we should maintain a healthy dose of skepticism reflecting the level of uncertainty in them.

Many, possibly most Americans believe in the Christian doctrine and believe in the existence and goodness of a monotheistic god. Such a faith has both positive and negative consequences.

Because of people's faith in god, many believers are engaged in doing good works. They participate in charitable activities by giving money, time, and talent to philanthropic organizations who provide food, clothing, and other essentials to people in need of help.

Most rational people, though they profess a faith in god and proclaim that god is in control of their lives, are smart enough not to believe it strongly. An Arab proverb exemplifies this practicality, "Trust in God but tie your camel tight." A Catholic Cardinal once said, "I pray as if everything depended upon God, but I work as if everything depends on me." Benjamin Franklin wrote, "God helps those who help themselves." Even those who profess to believe in heaven are not in a hurry to go there. If the word "hope" were substituted for faith and the word "wish" for prayer, statements concerning faith and prayer would be more accurate.

But there is a dangerous side to faith. The absolute certainty of one's beliefs with its unquestioned obedience to religious authorities, be they sacred texts or religious leaders, results in intolerance, dogmatism, and evil. We have seen this in the September 11,

2001 World Trade Center tragedy. Dogmatism and fanaticism can arise from any belief. Thus the twentieth century was full of holocausts and mass murders because of the fanatical beliefs of the followers of Nazism and Communism. In the case of religions, those who are convinced of the absolute sovereignty of god have no trouble in killing dissidents. Calvin, Zwingli, and many others were prepared to kill nonbelievers. Many, even today, are willing to kill those who do not believe as they do. Why shouldn't believers kill nonbelievers and sinners? After all, their gods and prophets have been in the damnation and killing business from the very onset. Love for god and the absolute belief in one's dogma often results in hatred of those who don't believe as you do.

Since faith is not based on logic or knowledge, how does one bring others to believe as you do? Religions employ a variety of techniques. These include witnessing or proclaiming one's belief in a certain deity or doctrine, doing good works, and living an upright and moral life as a role model to potential believers. It also includes displaying happiness in a newfound faith, developing a community of believers who give moral support to each other, and giving safe haven to believers. Bribery and promises of heaven and eternal happy afterlife; brainwashing; isolation from family and other nonbelievers; threats and acts of violence against nonbelievers; and the fear of going to hell and facing eternal damnation are also used. If one examines the breadth of religions, one can see all of these elements in action.   Loving gods employ moderate techniques; warlike aggressive gods tend to use force and violence to obtain converts.

One of the most effective techniques of bringing people to one's faith is to threaten them with an eternity of suffering.   Another technique utilizes brutality and force.   Al Capone found years ago that people are very obliging when they have a gun at their head. The threat of hell for eternity and the threat of death by an absolute ruler are big guns that most find hard to argue with.

People of faith generally discourage independent thinking by means of implicit or explicit threats.   Rote memorization is encouraged in place of critical thinking.   A schoolboy once remarked, "Faith is believing what you know ain't so."

Two boys were discussing death one day and one said, "When my mother dies she will go to heaven and when I die I will go to heaven and be with her."

"I don't believe that," replied the second boy.

"Oh yes I will.   When I die an angel will take me to heaven to see my mother."

"Do you really think that?" questioned the second boy.

The boy stopped, thought, and answered, "Well I don't really think it, but I believe it."

Religions know all the tricks of the trade to make people believe and distract them from critical thinking and evaluation.   Repetitions, wearing religious symbols, music, rituals, chanting, hope, and fear are all used.   H. L.

Mencken wrote, "Faith may be defined briefly as an illogical belief in the occurrence of the improbable."

As we gain greater knowledge of the world around us, it is harder and harder to believe in miracles, faith healing, and the possibilities of improbable occurrences.

Tolstoy's argument that life is meaningless without a belief in god and immortality is simply untrue. We see meaningful lives again and again in those who do not believe in immortality or gods. Many hold on to their religion because they think without it their lives would be meaningless, but meaning comes from within, not from an outer source. The only meaning religion and god can give people is to make them dot their i's and cross their t's so they will be sure to make the cut to get into heaven. However, the requirements for entrance are so vague and contradictory that no one can be sure they will make the cut. No one but you can give meaning to your life.

A popular mythology is that this great country was built on faith in god. It was not. People built it on faith in themselves and their fellow man. It is man, not god, who toils in the fields and factories. It is man, not god, who studies nature's ways and attempts to improve upon them. The belief that if one has enough faith one can get whatever one prays for, permeates man's illogical thinking.

If there were worldwide agreement on a single god and a full agreement on god's actions, desires, requests, demands, and activities, then a faith in such a god, even if it didn't exist, might serve humanity well. Until that agreement exists, religions must not be allowed to play a role in human affairs.

Believe what you will, but "Thou shalt not do evil in the name of the Lord."

There lives more faith in honest doubt,
Believe me, than in half the creeds.

Tennyson

Action and faith enslave thought, both of them in order not to be troubled or inconvenienced by reflection, criticism, and doubt.

Henry Amiel

RELIGION IS A COMPETITIVE BUSINESS

Religion is a man-made, man-supported, man-believed, commercial enterprise. Like any business, it is in competition for your attention, support, and money. Let no one forget that. Anything that is said or done which decreases the support of religion is a threat to the life of that business. We have only to observe the Catholic Church in its present crisis—the Church studiously ignored the evidence of sexual abuse of children by priests and ferociously fought to hide the evidence because it did not want to get bad publicity and lose business.

Competition between the major religions is keen but even that pales when compared with the competition between the sects of each religion. The Muslims seem to be doing a better job of convincing others, as Islam is growing faster than most of the other religions.

Those in public relations know that advertising, called evangelism and proselytism in religion, is more effective if they hand out free samples. The PR experts of religion know that the promises of everlasting happiness and the threat of an eternity of hell work well, especially among the superstitious and the uneducated. In some cases accepting a belief is the only way the recipient can obtain a benefit or get out of the ghetto.

Religion like any other business must convince the public, or at least its followers, that its brand is superior to all others. Otherwise, no customers. Religions are in cutthroat competition with one another and must spend an inordinate amount of time and effort coaxing money out of their constituents, much to the constituents' discomfort and economic hardship.

All business groups, including religions, must raise money to survive. Churches want you to believe that a donation to their church is a gift to god and that you will be well rewarded after you die. One can only imagine what the collection plate would look like if god decided to reward people during their lifetime rather than waiting until after they die. Many churches request a ten percent tithe from their members. Many secretive cults require and expropriate all of their followers' assets and belongings.

It is often necessary to destroy rivals in order to survive and prosper. Religions have learned to use hate to destroy the competition. Hatred of difference along with a fear of the unknown is a strong unifying emotion and frequently more lasting than love.

As a competitive business, religions and religious institutions should pay their way. The extensive and expensive holdings of religion should not escape taxation. The failure to pay taxes requires other taxpayers to shoulder a disproportionate share of the cost of government. The Constitution requires separation of church and state, but that does not mean that the church should not pay its fair share to support the state, which allows the church the freedom to exist.

Every sect is a moral check on its neighbor. Competition is as wholesome in religion as in commerce

Walter S. Landor

MIRACLES

The blind receive their sight and the lame walk, lepers are cleansed and the deaf hear, and the dead are raised up, and the poor have good news. Preach to them. – Matthew 11:5

Miracle as defined in Webster's dictionary is, "strange thing – to wonder at – wonderful – an event or action that apparently contradicts known scientific laws and is hence thought to be due to supernatural causes esp. to an act of God." Miracles, as commonly defined, are inexplicable or supernatural events and represent direct intervention of god in human affairs.

Jesus is credited with performing a number of miracles that are used to support the idea of his divinity. He raised the dead, healed people of various infirmities such as blindness and leprosy, cast out demons, walked on water, turned water into wine, and fed the multitudes. The power of performing miracles has also been exercised by others such as saints of the Catholic Church. Thanks to television and other media, we see and hear faith healers miraculously heal the lame who then throw away their crutches and walk triumphantly in front of thousands of wildly cheering believers.

Leprosy was a popular and visible target for miracle workers. It was hideous and scary to look at. People with leprosy were shunned because of fear that it was contagious. (It is only contagious with a long period of exposure to an infected leper.) Jesus allegedly cured one leper. Thousands of lepers who existed before and after the time of Jesus were untouched by this single miracle. Finally, a miracle worker with the name of Hansen discovered the cause of leprosy and man completed the miracle of controlling and curing the disease. Jesus' cure of one leper, even if true, was insignificant. Ironically, it is believed that the "Holy Crusaders" spread leprosy to Europe.

We have other types of miracles such as a person missing a flight and learning that the plane had crashed and he/she had escaped death. Another person who almost threw away a lottery ticket only to realize that it was a winning ticket. It was a miracle or god's intervention that the people in the incidents described above escaped death and won a fortune. For believers, it is not hard to see the hand of god in their lives or in the lives of others.

Most of us believe in miracles—we hope for a sudden twist of events so we can get a better job, buy a better home, or win a lottery. Miracles in that sense are simply wonderful, rare, fortuitous events. There is nothing wrong in hoping for miracles. On the other hand rare, unexplained, terrible things also happen in a lifetime. In the phrase of statistics these are called chance events. But chance events occur in one's life whether one believes in god or not. To use rare and unexplained events as proof of a supernatural power, whether attributed to god or the devil, is unreasonable.

The miracles of religion don't reflect favorably on god. For example, god's miracles show its capriciousness. If a terminal cancer patient gets well due to divine intervention, what does that say about those who die? Could it be that god doesn't love them? Why should an all-powerful and loving god choose only one person and leave out thousands of sufferers? Why not cure all of them? Why only one or two? What if a physician performs such miracles—randomly selects one patient and cures him, then tells all others to get lost? Would we think that physician is a good doctor or even a good person? If a human being walks on water or flies through air without the help of any mechanical devices, it means that god is bending the laws of nature to help that person. Why not let everybody else bend those laws and enjoy wonderful free-flying experiences?

In any case, religious miracles have certain characteristics. First, miracles are onetime, irreproducible events. Only the miracle-maker can perform that particular miracle and only at the time and place chosen by him. Nobody else, by definition, can repeat it. Second, objective and effective investigations by disinterested investigators are rarely allowed.

67

Miracles are not subjected to peer review and evaluation. The very thought of asking for verification is a sure sign of lack of faith and is not tolerated. Third, miracles directly affect only a few people—the person who is raised from the dead, the person who is cured of his leprosy, or the person who is given sight or the power of hearing. Fourth, if a miracle fails to take place, it may be the fault of the person who is seeking the miracle. That person may have lacked complete faith in the miracle performer. The lack of faith may not be evident to anyone other than the miracle performer, but god, Jesus, angels, or saints know of that lack of faith and act accordingly. Fifth, the news about miracles is usually anecdotal; if something is written about them, it is usually long after the miracle has taken place. The truth of miracles and their occurrences is justified by the fact that so many people believe them. All of them couldn't be wrong, could they?

We cannot run our present day life by means of miracles whether they come from god, Jesus, or some other anointed and blessed person. Modern day physicians routinely save the lives of thousands of people—not just one or two. They save the lives of people who come from all walks of life and from different economic and educational levels; people with different religious beliefs and no religious beliefs at all. It doesn't matter. If the physician has the appropriate know-how in treating, say, heart disease, most of his or her patients are treated and are likely to be helped. The skills acquired by physicians are subject to peer review. Techniques are adopted only when those skills are proven to be effective. Drugs, disease treatment methods, and medical equipment are documented so that all interested people can evaluate and verify them. Physicians pass on their experiences and learning through medical schools, internships, and residencies so that more physicians can learn the latest methods of treatment.

Modern day physicians cure many diseases with treatments that could not have been imagined even a hundred years ago. Polio has almost disappeared. Heart disease is less of a threat now than it was in the early twentieth century. Mechanical devices such as eyeglasses and hearing aids enhance our sight and hearing. Contagious diseases that used to kill millions of people are now a distant memory. Prostheses and wheel chairs enable people to move about with comparative ease. Many cancers are being cured, more ameliorated. Parenthetically, if god doesn't want people to shorten their lives, perhaps god doesn't want people to lengthen them either.

There really is no need to walk on water. If one is so inclined, there are thousands of models of boats one can purchase and enjoy the water sports. We can fly. We can pick up a phone and talk to people who are on the other side of the globe. We can turn the television on and hear the State of the Union message from the president as he is delivering it. Our agricultural scientists have improved the quality and output of our crops, which allows millions to escape hunger and famine. Any virgin, if she is so inclined, can conceive a baby – it is now a routine laboratory event. Some scientists even claim that they now have the capability to clone dead people; anyone with enough money can have their pets cloned.

In other words, our life is full of miracles. If Jesus or any of his disciples were to come back to earth, they surely would think they were in heaven. The life we lead now was unimaginable and unattainable even to the richest and most powerful Roman emperors.

We frequently interact with saviors. Every day, we work with miracle performers who touch many more people than the ancient saints and saviors were ever able to do. Our modern miracle-performers, who are everyday physicians, surgeons, physicists, chemists, and engineers, do not claim to be the sons or daughters of god. They do not insist that we believe that they are born of virgin mothers, and they do not tell us that we are going to hell if we don't show obedience to them or their fathers.

In reality, most alleged miracles are card tricks. Careful scientific investigations usually uncover fraud, self-deception, or just plain mistaken interpretations of the events. Where there is skeptical inquiry, miracles cease. It does seem a little odd that most miracles delay that wonderful trip to heaven and eternal bliss. Even Jesus and Muhammad didn't seem to be in a hurry to get to heaven.

Jesus' miracles, as well as those of many of the saints are unimpressive when compared to the needs of mankind or when compared to the miracles of modern society. Turning water into wine at a wedding feast while millions of people die from starvation is a rather trivial miracle. Curing one person when thousands are allowed to suffer is not much of a feat. Saving one person from death while 240 others are killed in an airplane crash doesn't say much about the wonders of god. A run of the mill physician saves more lives in his lifetime than did many of the saints, angels, and gods. In addition, the physician doesn't demand that you believe in a certain dogma, creed, or god before he treats you. God and miracle workers should be concentrating on preventing global holocausts, nuclear winters, and the deaths of innocent people.

A miracle supersedes the law of nature – of god's law if you will – but there is no proof that any such miracle has ever occurred. Miracles occur in the minds of religious believers and are simply an attempt to convince themselves and others that their god exists.

A question we should ponder is why we continue to celebrate thousand-year-old miracles of dubious nature rather than noticing and appreciating our everyday miracles and savoring life to the fullest?

Mysteries are not necessarily miracles.
                                        Goethe

Human credulousness creates miracles.

David Hume

Ignorance is the soil in which belief in miracles grows.

Robert G. Ingersoll -
From his speech "Superstition"

THE GOOD AND THE BAD OF RELIGION

As one considers the many religions, gods, goddesses, witches, sorcerers, and spiritualists, one must ask oneself if there is any good to come out of such beliefs. There is much to be admired in women and men who live worthwhile lives with or without the benefit of a supernatural power, but whether god and religion are relevant to mankind is another issue. What good can come from religion?

- Religion can give comfort and solace.
- Religion can give hope.
- Religion can teach good health habits.
- Religion can encourage charity and giving.
- Religion can encourage and stimulate education.
- Religion can teach worthwhile moral attributes.

■ Religion as a social institution can foster fellowship, friendship, and social activities.

■ Religion can make people believe that they are lovable and loved and that there is a god and a host of angels looking after their welfare.

■ Religion can allow people to bear the unfairness of life with the hope of an afterlife.

■ Religion can allow people to accept suffering with equanimity.

■ Religion can give some the satisfaction of knowing that god will judge their enemies in the next world.

■ Religion can give some the satisfaction of knowing that they and their loved ones are going to heaven.

■ The business of religion allows opportunities for employment, health care, and retirement benefits.

■ Tax-free religious buildings and property can be used for meetings, elections, and other public functions.

■ The church, as a social institution where people gather, can be a place for networking, gathering votes, building a practice, promoting a business, even meeting a future spouse.

During the days of slavery the church was the only place where blacks could congregate in relative safety. As a result, the black church leaders became the spokespersons for black interests.

It is only fair to concede that religion can be of value. The issue, however, is whether it does more harm than good. You should note that charitable, kind, generous, and loving people accomplished all of the good things listed above. Not a single one of them was accomplished by god.

We argue that we have other social institutions which can do a better job of solving humanity's problems than religion. We have in every society, charitable, kind, helpful, dedicated humans trying to better the lot of themselves and others. Humanitarianism exists with or without god.

Now let's take a closer look at the negatives of religions.

Religion can give solace and comfort, but only if you can convince yourself that there is a caring, loving god who is interested in your personal welfare and the welfare of your loved ones. As one looks at the unpredictability and randomness of nature and the suffering of humanity, that belief is difficult to accept. If god were to be believed, it would only have to give more blessings to its believers than to its nonbelievers. But we can plainly see that the rain falls on the believers and the nonbelievers alike. Does it really seem logical that god is going to sort them out after they die and reward the believers and punish others, when it hasn't chosen to do so in this life? Although religion can give comfort, solace, and hope, belief in god is not a requirement for those benefits. People with different belief systems can be comfortable as well as have hope. Except for the hope of immortality and heaven, believers have no more hope than nonbelievers. A positive attitude toward life does not depend upon religion.

Religion can teach good health habits. Certainly the prohibition of smoking, drinking alcoholic beverages, and the use of drugs has improved the health and increased the life expectancy of Mormons and Seventh-Day Adventists who stress those healthful habits. The problem with religion and its health teaching is that it is associated with god and sin. Another problem with the health habits of religion, as well as with god's sexual advice, is that you cannot measure god's feelings about those issues. Is it bemused, amused, or downright angry when you eat pork, shellfish, smoke, or refuse to have your child circumcised? You might assume that if god gave us the tobacco plant, it wanted us to smoke. Unfortunately, this is as valid an assumption as that it doesn't want us to smoke. Health education is of value on its own merit. People should practice healthy habits because those habits make their lives longer and more comfortable, not because they are expected to please god. There should be more sermons on the sin of gluttony with its attendant obesity and heart disease.

One of the most troubling areas where religion causes problems is the matter of sex.

Guilt is introduced, whereas a couple should experience the pleasure and joy of sexual activity without guilt. Now that we have the capability of protecting ourselves from unwanted pregnancies and sexually transmitted diseases, we should learn and teach safe sex. It is unfortunate that religions violate the privacy of consenting adults and attempt to dictate their very private lives. The guilt about sex prevents many parents, probably most, from even discussing it with their children.

It is especially harmful to society for religions to teach that god wants each and every sperm and ovum that get together to result in a child, no matter the economic, psychological, or parenting skills of the providers of that sperm and ovum – not to mention birth defects. That teaching and preaching of religion, although less believed and practiced today, greatly interferes with the humanitarian desire to have each and every child wanted and well cared for. The association of lust and parenting was a major defect in god's quality control.

Religion can encourage charity but women and men are charitable no matter their religious beliefs. Much of charity through the church is attached to indoctrination of their belief system. Religious charity can be as subtle as a club. Often the charity goes only to fellow believers or to those who accept their teachings. Charity should be done in the name of humanity, not god. Religions take money from the poor to sustain their own institutional activities. John Adams, as he traveled through

Spain en route to France noted, "Nothing appeared rich except for the churches – Nobody fat but the clergy."

Religions have encouraged and supported education. The Presbyterians were active in establishing schools in Appalachia and elsewhere, but historically some religions wanted an uneducated society except for the clergy. The Catholic Church was against anyone except their priests reading the Bible, as they believed it was necessary for the priests to interpret it for the common folks. Only the Pope is allowed to think. Today almost all of religious effort in education is based on indoctrination of the young to the belief of a particular sect. In fact, religions have withdrawn their support when the school or university did not sufficiently emphasize their religious beliefs. Some religious schools tolerate no teachings outside their faith. Much of home schooling in our society today is based upon indoctrination of the child into the dogma of his/her parents. Home schooling is also used to prevent the child from coming into contact with contrary or controversial views. Going hand in hand with religious indoctrination is the discouragement of critical thinking skills among children. Religious leaders are afraid to allow children to critically evaluate the world around them and come to their own conclusions.

What can we say about the worthwhile moral teachings of religion? Most of them are common sense and are in our own self-interest. People do not need a god to tell them not to lie, cheat, or steal. The issues of homosexuality, contraception, abortion, euthanasia, polygamy, suicide, capital punishment, and yes – even slavery, are and have been controversial and arguable. God has not sent us clear signals; it has only caused bickering and made it more difficult for humanity to decide what is best for society. Colonialism failed, not because of god's teachings that it was immoral, but because it became economically and militarily unsustainable. Likewise, social awareness that was brought on by the civil rights leaders of America and worldwide condemnation destroyed segregation. God's attitudes on moral issues are impossible to know.

The fellowship and friendship of religion can be worthwhile. Today however, most people have enough personal contacts that churches no longer play an important role in their social life. In communities where social activities are limited, the church offers fellowship that may not be readily available otherwise. With the many social, professional, charitable, cultural, and educational groups available today, most people do not need or even have time for church fellowship. In fact, churches are unable to meet all of the social needs of communities. Consequently, we now have government, secular nonprofit, and religious organizations working together to solve societal problems.

Finally, religion can help people deal with the unfairness of life. Creating a life of fairness was god's responsibility. We would think that only a devil would create an imperfect man and an unfair life for the good and the bad alike.

But we must accept the fact that life is unfair and we must deal with it as it is dealt.

It has been said that religion is the opiate of the masses. It does make some more amenable to the desires of the leaders. It will even make them more accepting of their own slavery and subjugation. The problem with the opium of religion is that it is used to stimulate and encourage activities that are antisocial. We have only to observe the many harmful deeds that are done in the name of god. If the opiate of religion cannot be controlled, it should be discontinued.

We maintain that religion does more harm than good. Consider the following:

■ Religion causes divisiveness, bigotry, and intolerance.

■ Religion interferes with science and the accumulation of knowledge.

■ Religion causes a fear of aging and death.

■ Religion supports immoral activities such as the subjugation of women and slavery.

■ Religion interferes with the establishment of a moral society by making absolutes out of polygamy, abortion, euthanasia, etc., without taking into account the needs of mankind.

■ Religion causes guilt over minor, inane, superstitious beliefs.

■ Religion causes fear and guilt when it tells women, men,

and children that god is watching their every move and they are going to hell if they don't fall to their knees and ask for forgiveness.

■ Religion causes a false sense of security when it convinces people that if they pray and have faith, god will bail them out of their difficulty.

■ Religion, with its obsession with sex, causes guilt, fear, sexual frigidity, and unwanted children.

■ Religion threatens all with hell except the members of their group.

■ Religion maintains that the devil causes evil instead of holding man responsible for his own evil.

■ Religion teaches that you can get to heaven no matter how evil you are, if you accept their prophet, god, or beliefs.

■ Religion allows the clergy to translate their moral beliefs into sins.

■ Religion preaches that all good things come from god when it is obvious good comes from parents, teachers, and many others.

■ Religion perpetuates ritual and superstition in the guise of pleasing god.

■ Religion limits the contacts of children and adults with

members of another faith.

■   Religion allows hatred of others who believe differently.

■   Religion allows people to kill and burn in the name of god.

■   Religion treats women differently than men in the affairs of the church.

■   Religion calls homosexuality an abominable sin when we do not know the cause of it.

■   Religion teaches that family planning is a sin and that god wants a baby every time an ovum and a spermatozoon come into close proximity.

■   Religion proclaims that AIDS, mental diseases, death, or any other calamity is the wrath of god or the work of the devil.

■   Religion preaches that the end of the world is coming and that god will murder us all at the end.

■   Religion tries to establish laws to enforce god's desires.

■   Religion tells a grieving family their loved one cannot go to heaven because he committed suicide.

■   Religion allows parents to deny their children medical care because they believe god is in control of disease and dying.

■   Religion makes excuses for their god by proclaiming that god works in mysterious ways.

■   Religion educates the young that there is only one god, their god, and all others are false.

■   Religion allows their followers to become smug, conceited, and overbearing because they and they alone, have the truth.

■   Religion blames satan for man's evil.

■   Religion devotes more time to the needs of god than to the needs of mankind.

■   Religion creates a god more cruel than man.

■   Religion discourages children from seeking truth by telling them that god does not like to be questioned and tolerates no discussion of its actions.

■   Religion gives god credit for man's accomplishments and good deeds.

All religions should examine their own dogma and discard those, which encourage hatred of people with other beliefs. All religions should repudiate and condemn their own scriptures when those scriptures advocate violence against people of other faiths. All religions should examine their own vocabulary and abandon and repudiate the words, phrases, and concepts that expose the people of other religions to hatred, violence, and death.

We frequently hear people give testimony that god, Jesus, Allah, Buddha, or some other prophet or religion helped them go from a wretched, unhappy life to a successful one. Through such testimonies, they demean themselves and belittle their own accomplishments. It wasn't god, religion, or a deity responsible; they did it on their own. In most instances, their motivation to stay sober or drug free or make a success for themselves was based on the self-realization that they would be happier and more comfortable if they made changes in their lifestyle. They should be justly proud of their accomplishments. To believe that god picked them for special benefits not afforded to all others is illogical. To believe that god helped one alcoholic or drug addict but not others is unreasonable.

As you can tell, this author believes there is more harm than good in the world's religions. Though religion may be of some benefit, the overall effect is deleterious to mankind. The benefits of religion are better attained by other means. Read any newspaper and see for yourself the many differences and conflicts created by the varying religions and their subgroups. Though many maintain that man needs religion, in reality man wants eternal happiness and only the fantasy of religion gives him that. Some people will insist that only religion meets the desire for eternal bliss, but so do heroin, illusions, fantasy, and delusions. It is false to believe that religion meets genuine needs that cannot be more honestly met by other means.

If religion were simply a soothing balm or a simple fantasy, no one need bother questioning it. As you study the history of religion you can plainly see that it is not a simple hope or fantasy. For those who have convinced themselves that they have pleased their god and are on their way to heaven, that fantasy may be comforting. However, some of the most devout believers have gone to their deathbed in doubt as to whether they had pleased a perfect divinity.

Susan B. Anthony wrote of the Bible, "I know of no other book that so fully teaches the subjection and degradation of women." As G.B. Shaw wrote, "There is nothing more dangerous than the conscience of a bigot."

Bertrand Russell wrote:

> I think all the great religions of the world – Buddhism, Hinduism, Christianity,   Islam,   and Communism – both untrue and harmful. It is evident as a matter of logic that since they disagree, not more than one of them can be true. With very few exceptions, the religion which man accepts is that of the community in which he lives, which makes it obvious that the influence of environment is what has led him to accept the religion in question.

Religion, like opium, puts you under the control of your supplier.

CHANGING RELIGIONS

Religion has changed. God has changed. The belief that god is unchangeable or that religion holds eternal truth from a divine being is untenable. Only those who are unwilling or unable to think logically can be blind to the many changes that have occurred. Bibles are filled with untruths, superstitions, and threats as well as the social mores of the day. Some falsehoods do little harm, but others do a great deal of harm to society as well as to the individual.

Superstitions, rituals, music, and chants are used to reinforce beliefs in the unbelievable. The crossing of one's self, sprinkling holy water, reciting the rosary, touching the front door before entering, and chanting that Allah is great are constant reminders that god exists and is unchangeable. But religious views on sexuality, homosexuality, and divorce are changing rapidly. So too are beliefs concerning birth control, family planning, and abortion. God said little about slavery that has existed since the beginning of man. The subjugation of women has been approved and perpetuated by god and its teachings. How anyone can believe a just god is against family planning, is for slavery, or is for the subjugation of women is beyond understanding. The morality of capital punishment is being debated today and god is on both sides. Even those harmful effects of religion are of lesser importance than the arguments, fights, and wars that are being waged over god today.

The changes in religion's dogmas have been slow but they are there for all to see. It took the Catholic Church hundreds of years to recognize that Galileo was correct when he stated that the earth was not the center of the universe. At one time the Church said the earth was flat. Magellan said about that untruth, "The church says the earth is flat; but I have seen its shadow on the moon, and I have more confidence even in a shadow than in the church." Martin Luther believed death was an expression of god's anger. Not many believe those religious "truths" today.

When it was believed and taught that the entire universe revolved around man and earth, man created a god in his own image with himself as the center of god's attention. When astronomy, geology, and mathematics proved that belief untrue you would think man had lost his security blanket. There still remains a repulsive smugness in those who believe a supreme being is interested in their welfare and devotes much thought to their actions.

Henry Ward Beecher noted in *Norwood*:

As men look back on nations in the olden time, and know that amid their fondest convictions they were in profound error – that their gods were myths, their histories half fables, and their theology a mere fiction, so now and then it came home to him with ghastly distinctness, that a time would come when men would look back upon him and his generation in the same manner.

That time has come.

We can see that religious beliefs are constantly changing. Whereas it was once believed that demons caused insanity and that they could be driven out of the mad by beating, we now know differently. If you do not believe religion is changing, think about the law in force 150 years ago in Maryland:

Be it enacted by the Right Honorable, the Lord proprietor, by and with the advice and consent of his Lordship's governor, and the upper and lower houses of the assembly, and the authority of the same:

That if any person shall hereafter, within this province, wittingly, maliciously, and advisedly, by writing or speaking, blaspheme, or curse God, or shall deny the Holy Trinity, the Father, Son, and Holy Ghost, or the Godhead of any of the three persons, or the unity of the Godhead, or shall utter any profane words concerning the Holy Trinity, or any of the persons thereof, and shall thereof be convict by verdict, shall, for the first offense, the offender shall be stigmatized by burning in the forehead with the letter B, and fined forty pounds. And that for the third offense the offender shall suffer death without the benefit of clergy.

Can you imagine such a law? This law is a good example of government controlling its people with religious dogma and fear. Many laws, similar to the law above, require all to believe and pay tribute to the prevailing god of the day. Virtually every social group has enacted such "religious" laws, which are frequently ignored but seldom repealed.

The nature of sin is evolving also. I am reminded of the middle-aged woman who was teaching a college physical education class in dance. She brushed off the gratitude of the students with, "Shucks, I learned to dance when it was a sin." Dancing, card playing, movies, drinking colas, the length of dresses, girls shaving body hair, and many other sins have gone by the way and more will follow. There was a time when drinking alcohol was a sin. In one of the discussions on alcohol, the author pointed out to his mother that Jesus turned water into wine. His mother didn't question the validity of Jesus' miracle but she simply replied, "That's true, but I would have thought a lot more of him if he hadn't."

Not only has religion changed in the past, it is changing every day as men and women become more educated and the pool of knowledge increases. The Emperor of Japan has gone from divine to human. Epilepsy, cholera, plague, as well as other natural catastrophes have gone from divine will to natural forces. God still gets the credit and the blame for natural disasters, but they too will be taken out of god's realm. Changes are occurring in every religion and in every sect of every religion. The following are examples and many more can be found in each religious group or subgroup:

Rabbis are not going to be able to convince Jews that wearing the kippah is very important in the scheme of things or that Yahweh still frowns on their eating pork. The Pope will not be able to convince women that god doesn't want them to use contraceptives or plan their families. The Pope will not be able to convince his cardinals and bishops that he has a direct line to god and they must accept what he says without dissension. God will surely tell the clergy it is permissible, even required, to allow women into the hierarchy of the church – and soon. Fundamentalists cannot continue to make educated, literate people believe that a man-written, multiple translated book written thousands of years ago with its internal contradictions, is infallible or that it is the literal word of god. Nor can religion continue to require women to submit to their husbands as property and chattel.

The British geologist Sir Julian Huxley said to a group of scientists attending the celebration of the 100th anniversary of Charles Darwin's *Origin of Species*:

> There is no longer either need or room for supernatural beings capable of affecting the course of events. The earth was not created. It evolved....So did all the animals and plants, including our human selves, mind and soul as well as brain and body.

The cosmos and everything in it is constantly evolving and changing. Religion, too, is constantly evolving. The change may be slow but an educated knowledgeable public will demand it or simply ignore the dogma – many do even today.

Religion Must Change:

Religions as well as god's attributes and actions must change if they are to continue to appeal to an educated, thinking public. Darwin's theory of evolution was questioned and disapproved of for years. Now, at least in most educated religious circles, it is accepted as part of god's divine plan. Few can believe that god created the universe in six days and then rested. Why does an all-powerful being require rest? If men and women worked a five-day week when the Bible was written, god would have created the cosmos in five days and rested two.

The church has always had a way of going slowly from untruth to truth, but only when the truth was obvious to most. Religions that do not change become extinct. There will always be gullible followers who will follow a charismatic orator and believe whatever he wants them to believe. The presence of UFOs, astrology, witches, sorcerers, fortune-tellers, spiritualists, and fundamentalists doesn't allow much optimism. On the other hand, most people have gone through Santa Claus, the Easter bunny, Charlie Brown's Halloween deity, and the tooth fairy without great difficulty. (Several of the author's friends confessed that they felt betrayed by their parents when they realized that Santa Claus didn't exist.)

Following are some of the ways religion will change or be discarded:

■ Religions will change as social changes occur. Religions will change as human knowledge increases. Widening horizons may allow the church to survive in a society of educated people but one thing is certain, the old dogmas cannot indefinitely continue to make people believe in a god who is more cruel and less forgiving than man.

■ Religion must change if there is ever to be a brotherhood

or sisterhood of men and women or if there is ever to be world peace. Religious strife was involved in every war in 2001. Religion cannot continue to be such a divisive force.

■ Religion cannot continue to make people believe that their suffering is due to sin and is god's will. The clergy may be able to convince some that suffering is due to sin, but they cannot convince many that an infant born blind and deaf is suffering because of its sin. Few will accept a god who punishes all of humanity because of Adam and Eve's sin. Not many will continue to believe that god murdered everyone except Noah and his family and that he will murder everyone again, except a chosen few, at the end of the world. Only cruel people can believe in hell. No humane person can believe that man will suffer eternally without any chance of atonement.

■ The clergy must continue to bring their god into modern times. God cannot continue to send lightning bolts or AIDS to punish mankind, especially when those indiscriminate bolts of lightning and the virus strike the good, the bad, the believers, and the nonbelievers – even newborn babies.

■ Religion will change god's sex. He must become gender neutral if he is to appeal to all. According to the males who wrote the Bible, god created them with lots of testosterone and then created females to take care of that problem. The author can just see the female version of the Bible – God created females first and then She created males to take out the garbage.

■ The clergy can insist that god's sense of justice, kindness, charity, and forgiveness transcends humanity's, but that will not satisfy those who believe god should be at least as kind and charitable as humans.

■ God must change from threatening hellfire and damnation to compassion, forgiveness, and caring. It is more accurate to call Christianity "Paulism" or "Constantinism" for it was Paul, obsessed with his own guilt, who found salvation in Jesus and championed him as a man turned into god. It was Constantine who converted to Christianity and then forced his belief on all he ruled. Without Paul and Constantine, it is unlikely that Christianity would have become a major player in the world of religions.

We must have sympathy for the problems of a changing religion. If a forgiving, friendly, kind god is created, the fear will be taken out of religion. Without fear, few will show up on the Sabbath and even fewer will tithe. But take heart; there is enough fear in life from anthrax, terrorism, and death to satisfy all of us. We really don't need the fear of an afterlife.

Be ye of good faith. Religion has changed, is changing, and must continue to change for a changing humanity.

There is nothing permanent except change
Heraclitus

STAY IN THE CLOSET

For those who agree with the logic, reasoning, and opinions expressed in this book, yet must depend on the public for income, votes, or good will, consider this advice. Stay in the closet.

When the author asked some of his close friends to evaluate his first book, *God.com – A Deity for the New Millennium,* several thought it was worthwhile and encouraged publication. Several others advised him to bury the manuscript, better still, burn it. All advised him to change his phone number to protect his family and himself from the hostility and intolerance of fanatical believers. They realized that, "Hell hath no fury like a man whose god has been criticized." When logic meets dogma, you can never predict the consequences.

If you had ties with a church in childhood but no longer have, it is better that you continue to name that church as your religious preference. It will save many explanations. If you profess "none," you may be labeled an atheist with all the pejorative notions and feelings that go with that label. Many religious folks have been taught that you cannot be moral without religion and a fear of god. They will look down their nose at you if you do not profess to believe in god or profess to have a religion. Some will try to convert you to their wonderful, loving religion. Others will try to make your life a hell, as they can't wait for their god to make your eternity a hell.

This author finally worked up the courage to put his thoughts on paper. It should be noted that he did not do it until his children were grown and out of the nest, his financial future secure, and the need of public approval was not a prime consideration. The author was in a position to withstand the heat. However, he cannot recommend that those who are younger and more dependent on public opinion come out of the closet. If it were not for the author's strong opinions on the harm resulting from religion, neither this book nor *God.com* would have seen the light of day. Of course, this author has also been known to suffer from mural dyslexia – the inability to read the handwriting on the wall.

Even today, in North Carolina, South Carolina, Maryland, Arkansas, Mississippi, Pennsylvania, Tennessee, and Texas, it is against the law for an atheist to hold public office. As more people emerge from the closet, the majority will come to realize that those who do not believe in the supernatural can be worthwhile moral citizens just as can gays, lesbians, blacks, Jews, women, and other minority groups. As time goes on, perhaps more nonbelievers will feel safe to emerge into the daylight. The prejudice against nonbelievers is as pernicious as the prejudice against any other minority.

One has only to observe the fates of Benjamin Franklin and Thomas Paine to see the difference between keeping your mouth shut and expressing your opinion. They both had similar beliefs. Ben was advised to tone down his criticism of religion and did so, and died with honor. Tom continued to publicly question religion and died in ignominy. Not much has changed in over two hundred years in this respect. Even those in the closet should get in a barb now and then or ask a sensible question when the religious expert expresses the harmful dogmas of his religion. As science and knowledge expands and as more people become educated, more will be able to gain insights into religion, god, nature, and life. It is a sign of gross intolerance when a nonbeliever cannot express his opinion in a society of believers.

There are many dropouts from the dogmas of religion. Those who study comparative religion recognize the many differences and inconsistencies. Others, who find they cannot believe the dogmas of their religion, drop out or shop around for a group they can feel comfortable with. As time goes on, more and more may be able to fearlessly explore alternate dogmas or even profess non-belief in a god without worrying about their personal safety and reprisal. Not yet for most people.

Freedom of speech is one of the greatest gifts of our American democracy. In a society where the majority believes in a god, the freedom that questions or criticizes god may come at considerable personal cost. One must weigh the risks and as Harry Truman said, "If you can't stand the heat, stay out of the kitchen." If Bishop John Shelby Spong, a believer and author of *Why Christianity Must Change or Die* thinks he has problems as a "believer in exile", he should appreciate what nonbelievers in exile must suffer. One must always take into account people's beliefs, whether they are true or not. Successful politicians, public speakers, even writers, are well aware of this. There has never been an avowed atheist elected to public office.

Thirty million Americans have no specific religious affiliation but far fewer will admit to having no religion. Still fewer will criticize even the most ridiculous description of god's actions, wishes, desires, and commands. It is politically incorrect to criticize anyone's god, no matter how silly or harmful it is. Most do not want to suffer the fate of David Hume, the Scottish philosopher, who was criticized unmercifully when he wrote of his disbelief in miracles and immortality. When Hume applied for the chair of moral philosophy at Edinburgh in 1744, his objectors alleged heresy and atheism, which then and even today was enough to keep him from getting the job. Unsuccessful in his quest for the job, he left Edinburgh.

One can understand how a frightened, uneducated person might create a god or a goddess. One can imagine oneself in Africa five thousand years ago struggling to survive with predators, enemies, floods, sickness, and droughts. There is little knowledge and few support systems. One then creates a god to give psychological sustenance and hope for the future.

One can understand how a vengeful person could create a hell for his enemies and for those who disagree with him, but most cannot understand how any humane person can continue to believe in a god who murders, kills, aborts fetuses, and wreaks havoc on mankind with disease, pestilence, and natural disasters. Many do not believe in such a god but they are reluctant to speak out because of childhood fear and an unwillingness to take on the dogmatic intolerance of the believers. They follow a wise admonition – *Don't get in a pissing contest with a skunk.*

All of us live within a social group. We must abide by the rules, mores, and laws of that group. (The Dixie Chicks can attest to this.) The members of a Jewish, Christian, or Muslim society are expected to conform. If one does not, one is criticized and ostracized. When religion is in complete control, you may even be killed for expressing your opinion. For those who are dependent upon the goodwill of the public, it may be better and safer to stay in the closet.

Nonbelievers remain quiet for several reasons. Most do not want to start an argument about religion, sex, or politics. Some feel that religion may perform a worthwhile service even if it is untrue. Some people think that humanity needs the fear of god to control mankind's evil intentions. Some others are concerned with tearing down a belief system without an adequate replacement. Others, as a point of etiquette, do not want to start an emotional discussion about religion. There are times when one allows people to believe what they want to believe. For example, what does a surgeon say just before an operation when a patient asks him, "Are you a Christian?" Or what does one do when their hairdresser or butcher starts a diatribe on god and what god wants? Little white lies are frequently required to oil the machinery of interpersonal relationships.

Why should people get angry with someone who doesn't believe in an all-knowing, all-powerful god? Nonbelievers don't get angry with those who believe in such a god, though they may be disappointed and frustrated from time to time.

Many great philosophers have stayed in the closet. Rene' Descartes published his works anonymously as he wanted to avoid conflict with the church. Most people will not share their true beliefs publicly. In fact, many politicians in American public life walk around ostentatiously with a Bible in their hands. Family members often will not express their true beliefs to the believers in their own family. Even Mark Twain, the great cynic, would not discuss religion with his believing wife. The saying, "You can't handle the truth" is reason enough not to express truth.

Thomas Jefferson compiled what he believed to be the sayings of Jesus and it became known as *The Jefferson Bible.* He cut out many supernatural elements from the apostles' accounts of the life and teachings of Jesus.   But he kept that Bible to himself for years. He said, "Religion is a matter which solely lies between man and his God, that he owes account to none other for his faith or his worship."   *The Jefferson Bible* was not published until 1904, over a century after his death.

Skepticism, agnosticism, and atheism arouse displeasure in many and may interfere with one's position in a society of believers; a good reason for remaining quiet except when harmful, hateful views are expounded.   Many have stopped thinking, asking, or caring about god, as they do not believe that god is relevant to human behavior; but only a few carry the banner of atheism.   Believing or not believing in god should be a private and personal matter.

Most believers are unable to describe their god and explain its actions or inactions without making excuses.   If one were to point out the many excuses made for god, some people would strike back in hostility.   A fear of god since childhood will not allow many to consider alternatives to their dogma.   If religion did not do so much harm, we could ignore it. Many do anyway.

This author contends that humanism is an   adequate   replacement   for   religion. Humanism cannot compete with a god who will give you an eternity of happiness or an eternity of hell, but humanism can make your life and that of your fellow man more pleasant.

Things have come to a pretty pass when religion is allowed to invade the sphere of public life.
                                        Lord Melbourne

SOCIETY UNDER GOD'S RULE

The United States is the intellectual heir to renaissance, reformation, and the stunningly farsighted fundamental freedoms envisioned by the founders of the country. The culmination of these events for us is the Bill of Rights, which gave us freedom of religion and some freedom from religion.

Thomas Jefferson and James Madison 200 years ago saw the dangers of a Virginia bill authorizing tax support for churches. Madison wrote the *Memorial and Remonstrance against Religious Assessments* and was successful in defeating the proposed law. Among the points Madison made were:

> Those who do not believe are taxed to support those who do.

> An established clergy is always a convenient aid to rulers who want to subvert the liberties of the citizens.

Centuries of the legal establishment of a church produced pride and indolence in clergy, ignorance and servility in the people, superstition, bigotry, and persecution in both.

If government can establish Christianity to the exclusion of all other religions, it can later establish one sect to the exclusion of the rest or force a citizen to support such sect as it may choose.

Fortunately for all of us, Jefferson and Madison were successful in keeping government and religion separated. Although they were able to give us freedom of religion, freedom from religion would have to come much later. Society would not accept freedom from religion then, nor will it now.

The freedoms of religion and from religion are important for our society. Society under god's rule is more correctly a society under the rule of the clergy. Such a society is inimical to democracy, intellectual freedom, right to privacy, civil liberties, and the right to live in a peaceful world.

Civil society:

American constitutional government separated civil from religious society. Civil society as fashioned by the founders of the country, allowed its citizens to live in freedom, including the freedom to practice the religion of their choice. They further promised not to interfere with the right of religious freedom and recognized the right of its citizens to hold diverse religious beliefs. Government does not infringe on that right except when gross harm occurs to others. Religious society, in contrast, does not recognize the right of people to hold beliefs that are different from the officially sanctioned beliefs.

We can thank our lucky stars that our forefathers had the wisdom to understand the dangers of religion and the courage to separate church and state. That gave its citizens some freedom from religion. John Adams, in writing about himself and his fellow framers of the Constitution said, "It will never be pretended that any persons employed in that service had interviews with the gods, or were in any degree under the influence of Heaven." He further added that the government was "founded on the natural authority of the people alone, without a pretense of miracle or mystery."

Religious power and imposition is exercised in subtle as well as obvious ways. It was common at one time in America for the clergy to preach and teach school children that they would go to hell if they did not believe and obey the clergy. They terrorized children with gory details of hell. Non-believing or atheist children were and are forced to pray to a god they didn't believe in. Even today people are required to swear on the Bible when they are called to courts as witnesses, plaintiffs, or defendants. Many communities enacted laws prohibiting businesses to open on Sundays. Grocery stores are not allowed to sell alcoholic beverages on Sundays. Even now many organizations, which have nothing to do with religion, start their meetings with religious invocations.

Believers are now in the process of placing IN GOD WE TRUST on school walls and other public places even though no sensible person would leave his health and welfare up to god. A vocal majority is now decrying the removal of UNDER GOD from the Pledge of Allegiance. The phrase, under god, was put in the Pledge in 1954 to prove to those ungodly Russians and Chinese that we were more moral than they. The insistence of Under God and In God We Trust is simply the effort of religion to perpetuate their faith and force all to recognize their god. It should be obvious to all that if an all-powerful, all-knowing being exists, everybody and everything is subject to and under its control. It can slap us down or raise us up whenever it desires.

We are now in the midst of a discussion as to whether taxpayer's money should be given to religious institutions to "do good". In spite of the inefficiencies of governments and bureaucracies, tax money should not be allotted to those who are working for god. There are many nonsectarian, charitable, nonprofit groups who are working for mankind that can use taxpayer money to good advantage; faith-based funding is neither wise nor necessary. God is capable of doing its own good if it is so inclined. Tax money should not be given to religious groups whose primary concern is in perpetuating their faith. If a church wants to require everyone to pray and accept their god before giving food to the starving, that is their right, but taxpayer's money should not be used in this way.

We are fortunate in our American society that we can fight the encroachment of religion on civil society by using the court system. People can appeal to the courts to obtain redress. Even though it may take numerous attempts, eventually civil freedoms start asserting themselves through the court rulings. On the other hand, there are a number of societies where church and state are not separated. In those societies, people who hold beliefs that are contrary to the state-sanctioned beliefs suffer loss of civil liberties and sometimes their lives. In Spain under the rule of General Franco, only Catholics could hold public office or be officers in the military.

The Supreme Court of Bangladesh, an Islamic country, ruled that all Fatwas (religious decrees imposing the death sentence) were illegal and banned. They further ruled that those seeking such "justice" in that manner were in defiance of civilized law and must be punished for incitement to murder. Clergy who encourage their followers to unlawful acts should be prosecuted for aiding and abetting. It may not be against the law to shoot off your mouth when you don't know what you are talking about, but it is against the law to incite others to perform unlawful acts. Recently, a Muslim cleric in London was convicted of inciting others to murder and for stirring up racial hatred. One should not be able to hide behind the cloak of religion to preach hatred and violence against others.

Just imagine what our country would be like if the Catholics or Mormons or Seventh-Day Adventists or Jehovah's Witnesses or Baptists had their way and enforced their beliefs by law on everyone. All can see what the Muslim countries are like and one can imagine what Israel would be like if the ultra-Orthodox Jews were to gain control. That doesn't imply that a society run by atheists, agnostics, humanists, even Unitarians, would be without discussions, disagreements, and fights, but at least those fights would not be about god's wishes and commands.

Hindu fundamentalists recently pulled Valentine cards from Indian stores and burned them. Muslim clerics banned the same from Iranian stores. Surely, all who read a newspaper can see that the many religions and the thousands of gods created by people will never be able to work in harmony for mankind. Religion must be removed from the equation of humanity if there is ever to be any possibility for peace. The "Prince of Peace" would better be called the "Prince of Discord".

Democracy:

Kemal Ataturk, the father of modern Turkey, lifted a backward Muslim country into reform and democracy. First he had to put down religion. He once said to a reporter, "I have no religion, and I wish all religions at the bottom of the sea.... My people are going to learn the principles of democracy, the dictates of truth, and the teaching of science. Superstition must go." By the time of his death Islam was no longer the official State religion of Turkey. Turkey is the only Muslim country where a semblance of democracy exists today. It would just be another Muslim dictatorship state had not Ataturk put religion in its place.

If Iraq is to become a more free and democratic society, the clergy must be kept in the mosques and out of the government. You will never see or hear of a free people under god's rule. There has never been a free democratic government ruled by the JCM god and there never will be. The world does not need another Islamic, Christian, or Jewish theocracy.

Intellectual freedom:

Societies under god's rules are inimical to intellectual freedom – the freedom to think, the freedom to write, and the freedom to explore the natural world. The fight against evolution is a case in point. Science in general and evolution in particular, start with the assumption that most of the things we observe in nature can be explained without resorting to a magical supernatural power. Evolution, for instance, does not start with the assumption that god created the world in six days and that all living forms were created by god just as we see them today. Evolution proposes that all biological species, including man, evolved over time and that man is evolutionarily close to apes. All these propositions directly contradict the myth of Genesis. Fundamentalist Christians not only don't want their children to learn about evolution, they don't want any other child to learn about it either. For almost a century, American society, despite its stunning scientific and technical advances, has had to fight the fundamentalist's beliefs. Battles for the minds of children give rise to mutant theories such as creation science and intelligent design.

These intellectual battles are continuing as the religious establishment in the United States throws its economic and political weight against scientific advances such as the research in genetics, cloning, and anything that might possibly be connected with that dirty word, sex.

In many theocratic societies, critical analysis of religious scriptures and foundations is forbidden. In fact, there are instances where the writers who go against the views of the religious establishment have lost their lives.

Right to privacy:

Consensual sex, procreation, and women's right to control their bodies are among the favorite areas of oppression for the religious establishment. The laws against gays, lesbians, and private sexual activities between consenting adults are primarily religious laws.

The Catholic Church and others oppose abortion, which is an understandable position, even if wrong. However, they then go on to deny the right to practice birth control, which would reduce abortions. Likewise, they oppose drugs that prevent the fertilization of ova. All of these policies leave women in a catch-22 situation—everything they do is a sin and the only solution is the one offered by the church, which is no solution at all. In this situation one is reminded of the old riddle: What do you call people who practice the rhythm method of contraception? Answer: You call them parents. It is interesting to speculate as to why religion and god are so "hung up" on sex.

Peace among nations:

What do you suppose the religious leaders taught those young men who hijacked the planes and killed thousands of innocent women, men, and children? That is religion in action. One of our evangelists said the victims of that terrorist attack were sinners and that god had punished them. That also is religion in action.

The September 11, 2001 attack on the World Trade Center clearly revealed the dangers of the hatred and intolerance that religions promote. Thousands of innocent victims died in the attack and thousands more of the families suffered irreparable harm from the loss of loved ones. The investigations that came after the attack revealed that Muslim clerics in countries such as Germany, England, and Pakistan aided and abetted this gruesome act. Islamic clergy provided training, money, and theological justification to carry out this heinous deed.

The last part of the twentieth century saw many conflicts where religious hatred was the underlying cause. Religions play a major role in the conflicts of man. Each religious group or sect insists upon its own infallibility. Muslims were butchered in one conflict, Christians in another, Jews in yet another, and so on. All of these victim groups remember the atrocities committed against them and wait for their turn to avenge them. The cycle goes on and on. If there is peace in heaven, you can be sure that no discussion of religion will be allowed.

Despite every religion's claim that it is for peace and love, they seem powerless to stop this carnage and put an end to the cycle of violence. What makes this madness so scary is that biological, chemical, and nuclear weapons are within the reach of the religious fanatics. These weapons, along with the theological justifications for "Jihad" and "Holy Wars", mean more destruction and misery in the future. We can blame religion for being used for evil and as an excuse for violence.

If we were really a Christian nation, we would sell all of our military assets and give the money to the poor. Of course we would be conquered and killed, but what the heck, we'd all go to heaven and live happily ever after. That is the perfect answer to WWJD. (What would Jesus do?)

Wiley Miller in his cartoon, *Non Sequitur*, showed two early men in a cave, one drawing a mural of men fighting. The second man says, "No No No – First we invent religion to justify our actions. *Then* we invent war." Politicians are experts at using religion to get their way.

Kings, queens, and emperors have ruled by divine right. That divine right was always backed by force. As Voltaire is reported to have said, "God is always on the side of the heaviest battalions." God seemed to be on Germany and Japan's side for some time, before finally siding with the Allies in WWII after thousands of young men were killed. One would think god would decide early in a war who is right and who is wrong, saving countless lives. Both George W. Bush and Saddam Hussein claimed that god was on their side. Unfortunately, god didn't seem to be on the side of some of the young GIs nor on the side of hundreds of innocent Iraqis who were caught in the crossfire.

Hans Küng pointed out in his book *Christianity and the World's Religions,* that there could be no world peace without religious peace. All of us can see the hostility between religions as well as the hostility between the sects of the major religions. You may conclude as did Küng that what is needed are ecumenism and more ecumenical dialogue. Or you may conclude that what is needed is a replacement of religion with humanism. You may even conclude that we simply need civility. Not long ago an Anglican was visiting the Vatican. A Cardinal told him, "It is about time we stopped treating each other as Christians and started treating each other as gentlemen."

Conclusion

You cannot have a moral, just, legal system under the law of god; you will only end up with man-made laws alleged to have come from god. God's laws, more accurately god's vague directions, do not come up to mankind's sense of fairness and justice. While god's laws are carved in stone, man's laws can be changed as problems arise. The ability to change laws is a great safeguard against theological tyranny. In answer to a history question, "Why did the

Puritans come to this country?" a young student wrote, "To worship in their own way and make other people do the same."

All sorts of laws concerning abortion, euthanasia, cloning, embryo research, birth control, sexual activity, suicide, slavery, subjugation of women, and marriage and divorce, will be enacted in a society under god. It will be claimed that they are god's commands. Unfortunately, we cannot verify the claim that god is communicating directly with the lawmakers but we can insist that god enforce its own "laws".

God should be excluded from mankind's decisions until it issues and enforces clear and definite instructions that all can hear and understand.

We admit of no government by divine right the only legitimate right to govern is an express grant of power from the governed.

William Henry Harrison

Does It Matter

In spite of books such as this, god is going to be around for a long time. There is a lot of time, effort, money, and lives invested in god. The fear that has been created in the name of the JCM god will not be easily overcome. Despite our logical thinking, experience, and education, we still stop in our tracks when we a see a black cat crossing our path; we still knock on wood; we still carry things like horseshoes, rabbits' feet, and lucky tokens for good luck. In the same manner, the fear of god will continue, even as we know better. Many of us will continue to wager as Pascal did and decide that it is better to believe, or at least say we do, and be wrong, than not to believe and be right.

The question one must ask is: does it matter what people believe or want to believe about god? Here we are questioning the existence of god, heaven, hell, and the soul—when perhaps these things make absolutely no difference at all. If there is a god, it is doing its own thing, whatever that "thing" is. Whether or not there is a god, it is obvious that in the end man must depend upon himself and his fellow man for his continued survival, comfort, and happiness. If there is or isn't a god, we still must depend on our fellow human beings. With or without god, nothing is going to change and the cosmos will go on its merry way, no matter what. Though many people believe in the power of prayer, all have found better results by taking concrete steps to achieve what they want rather than praying and wishing for it. If prayer worked we would have had world peace long ago.

You might say, "Let it be." Several of our friends have advised this. They maintained, and rightly so, that people have been questioning and arguing about god for thousands of years and this book isn't going to change anything. In reality, it doesn't matter if people believe in god or not, as long as no harm is done to innocent people. What is the harm of a wish, prayer, or fantasy? But here is the rub. God and religion often are harmful not only to the individual but also to societies. If there were no harm from religion, this book and others like it need never be written.

To answer the question – yes, religion matters. Religion matters not so much for the good it does, but for the harm it is responsible for. It does not matter what an individual believes if he takes no action based on that belief but it most decidedly matters when 19 Muslims slam into the World Trade Center killing thousands, all in the name of and for their god.

■ It matters when Jerry Falwell says that thousands were killed because man has sinned and god is just warning us.

■ It matters when charismatic orators preach that AIDS was sent by god to punish mankind.

■ It matters when slavery is supported, abortion providers are killed, and witches are burned, all in the name of god.

■ It matters when god tells women that they should not use contraceptives for family planning.

■ It matters when parents withhold lifesaving medical care from their children on instructions from god.

■ It matters when people, including innocent children, are threatened with a god who will send them to hell if they question scriptures or think independently.

■ It matters when people are overwhelmed with guilt for something they are not responsible for.

■ It matters when gullible people are convinced to do evil by spellbinding orators.

■ It matters when people are persuaded to give up their worldly goods, even their lives, to follow the spellbinder to the "holy land". Then when the "holy leader" commits adultery with his followers, it matters.

■ It matters when the clergy uses their position to abuse children and others.

■ It matters when Jews fight Muslims; when Catholics fight Protestants; when Shiites fight Sunnis; when Hindus fight Muslims.

■ It matters when ethnic and political differences are exacerbated by religions – as between the tribes in Africa or between the Catholics and the Serbs of Yugoslavia or between the Catholics and the Protestants in Ireland or between the Muslims and the Jews in the Mideast or between the Hindus and the Muslims in South Asia.

■ It matters when people murder because god demands it.

■ It matters when god sanctions the subjugation and mistreatment of others based on their race, color, gender, or sexual orientation.

■ It matters when god sanctions wars and related brutalities.

It may not matter whether religion is true or not but it certainly matters when people believe it and act on that belief. It may not make much difference if an individual believes in astrology, UFOs, aliens, spirits, witches or sorcerers, but when people band together and support harmful causes such as noted above, it matters greatly. It doesn't matter if religion functions as an opiate but it decidedly matters when it is used as a stimulant and a sword.

If Osama bin Laden were acting alone, he would be a danger to a few, but as the leader of a group of dedicated and fanatical followers, he is a danger to many. Organized religion has always been more dangerous than one deluded individual.

It may not be possible or even wise for people to give up their fantasies, illusions, hopes, and dreams, but society should not allow them to harm others based on their beliefs.

In matters of religions, it is very easy to deceive a man, and very hard to undeceive him.
Pierre Bayle

MORALITY

Societies survive by acknowledging, accepting, and adopting a code of behavior. This code of behavior consists of simple guidelines such as take care of your parents, children, and other members of your family; treat your neighbor with courtesy and kindness as you would have them treat you; respect others' rights to their property and privacy; do not steal or cheat; be truthful and honest; do not commit violence or murder. These guidelines, with or without Moses, underlie all human societies.

One question that confronts us is where do these guidelines or commandments come from?

Judeo-Christian tradition claims that god gave the Ten Commandments to Moses and that these are god's directives for all to live by. God's commandments thus form the basis of our moral code. These commandments are claimed to be inviolable and unchanging commands from god. Since these commandments came directly from god, morality and religion have been linked together ever since. Religious believers assert that there is no morality without god and religion and that if man would only follow those simple rules, humanity would be saved and god would be pleased. Violators of these commandments obviously would go to hell unless they proclaim faith in god just in time to save their souls.

Although some maintain that the Ten Commandments form the basis of western law and jurisprudence, such is not the case. The Ten Commandments are much too simplistic and naive to be the basis for a system of justice. One should not accept the claim that morality is god-given.

As you look at the Ten Commandments, you can see they are a mixture of religion and morality. The religious portion of the commandments, for example, thou shalt not pray to any other god, reveals god's jealousy and intolerance. That commandment would lead one to believe that the one and only god was concerned about rivals. Benjamin Franklin excluded all of the commandments that dealt with god and kept only those which pertained to the welfare of humans. So should we.

We can see that it wasn't god who was afraid or jealous of other gods; it was man who created god and then insisted that only it was to be accepted and worshipped. It is not god who is jealous and demands constant attention and adoration; it is those who want all to believe in their god. It is humans who insists that their concept of the deity be accepted by all others and insist that their god shall have no competition.

Evolution of morality:

The rules of morality, despite the claim that god's commandments are unchanging and inviolable, have changed throughout history. When the movie *Gone With the Wind* was released, people were shocked when Clark Gable said, "Frankly my dear, I don't give a damn." Damn was a word of blasphemy. Television, movies, and press practiced censorship and prohibited the use of words, even the word "pregnancy". Today in contrast, there is little shock in watching *Sex and the City.* One can readily see the changes in the morality of language and sex. Sex hasn't changed; male lust hasn't changed; female desires to procreate and have families haven't changed but false modesty, prudishness, and guilt have changed. The idea of what constitutes moral behavior is constantly changing.

Neither god nor its followers have been consistent in upholding the moral code of the Ten Commandments. Many religions in the past supported and upheld slavery, prohibited intermarriage between the races and between the followers of different religious sects, and encouraged the killing of heretics and witches. The Biblical god demanded the killing of Abraham's firstborn son by Sara. Fortunately for firstborn sons, we no longer condone the sacrificing of one's child to god. Even today many religions encourage the harassment of homosexuals and the subjugation of women.

We are now repelled by the cruelty and
inhumanity of slavery, segregation, and Jim
Crow laws. We are becoming more tolerant
towards intermarriages of various kinds. We
continue the struggle to decriminalize
homosexuality and improve the civil rights of
homosexual men and women.

Surely one can see that god's
commandments have evolved over a long period
of time and that the beliefs held by Christians
and others have changed as well. Oh sure, god
has been pretty consistent that man shouldn't
lie, murder, steal, or commit adultery, but those
admonishments have been present for as long
as people have lived in groups. They are
necessary for survival in a group. Even lying,
killing, and stealing have so many shades of
meaning that the simple "thou shalt nots" are
meaningless as can be seen by the complexity
of our laws and court decisions.

Problems with rules of morality:

There are other aspects to the moral
commandments. There is conflict among the
moral rules and there is a gradual separation
of moral code into legal and ethical rules.

War is an example where god's
commandments are violated for a greater good.
In wars, killing is expected, encouraged, and
rewarded. Lying, in order to mislead the
enemy, is permitted. So, the simple commands
of "Thou shalt not kill" and "Thou shalt not lie"
evolved into modern morality where exceptions
are allowed for the sake of justice. It should be
remembered; victors determine whether a war

is just or unjust. WAR may be a mnemonic for Winners Are Right.

But a more intractable problem in our modern life is the conflict between ethical and legal conduct. Tax and accounting laws are so complex that businesses can do something legal even though it is unethical. For instance, in recent corporate scandals, corporate executives sold their stock, knowing that their corporations were on the verge of collapse while at the same time prohibiting their employees from selling stock in their retirement accounts. It may be perfectly within the law to do that, but the result of this legal behavior resulted in employees losing their retirement money and executives reaping millions.

You can see that the conflict between what is legal and what is right is present in all walks of life. Consider the present dilemma concerning capital punishment. First, god itself is unsure of its commandments. "Thou shalt not kill," says Exodus 20:13 but Numbers 35:16 says, "The murderer shall surely be put to death." Take your pick. Those who speak for god can be on either side. But there is another vexing problem. The legal system is so riddled with errors and racial and economic bias, an innocent man can be tried on charges of murder and be condemned to death. On the other hand, a rich person who can afford expensive legal counsel can go free despite the fact that he committed murder.

The point is that the conflicts among moral codes and the separation of moral code into legal and ethical codes end up being an unpredictable lottery—lucky people avoid the consequences of their moral transgressions and unlucky people can be caught and punished for things they did not do.

Our shrinking world and the increasing population is resulting in the need for environmental morality. In Biblical days with a small population, all that need be said was, "The solution to pollution is dilution." Not today where the large increase in the population is causing a host of problems that require a whole new set of environmental rules. These new rules will be translated into morality and will be necessary for humanity to survive in a large urban society. Land use, pollution, the care of animals, littering, disposal of man's garbage and sewage, will and must become moral issues for human happiness and survival. Man, for the benefit of mankind, will establish that morality. Though the religious experts may argue over whether Jesus would drive a SUV or not, a more logical eco-morality must be established by society. Since the world's social groups are so different, that emerging morality will vary, sputter, and stall. Religious morality with its vague, poorly communicated, unchangeable dogma is not sufficient for human needs. As eco-morality staggers forth, we must make certain that it is not established by an emotional, pushy, irrational minority to the detriment of the majority.

So much for the unchanging laws of god.

Morality is based on consensus:

In truth, morality was never established from on high. It was not written on stone or golden tablets and relayed to mankind by the prophets. It has always been and always will be established by man for the benefit of humankind. That is why we have debates about issues such as slavery, abortion, homosexuality, capital punishment, and human embryo research. Only after long debate do we come to a consensus on these issues and only then do we establish rules of morality. Because god did not impose this consensus and because free people established it, we are free to revisit the issue and come to a different decision at a later date. Thus, setting rules of morality is a human activity that is subject to error and revision. Morality must be decided by humanity, not by a remote god who lacks communication skills.

We should not minimize the importance of morality. Without a moral code and a legal system based on it, brute force will rule. Morality is the best way to keep brute force in check. But it is humans who must establish and enforce morality. God is on the sidelines.

Man's morality is self-interest in his own welfare. Morality is necessary to protect and nurture the members of a human society. Usually it is the most good for the most people. The technological advances in transportation and communication, which were completely unknown to the ancient gods, require new and different moral guidelines. Every social group has its own moral code, but all are based upon self-interest.

The attention, time, money, and human resources that are expended to satisfy an omnipotent god's desires detract from the concerns and resources we should expend on our fellow man. Rousseau wrote in *Confessions of Faith,* "As for dogmas which influence neither actions nor morality.... I never trouble myself about them." More should stop troubling themselves with the needs of an all-powerful being. An all-powerful, all-knowing being cannot have needs, wants, or desires that it cannot satisfy on its own.

Many, from Jefferson to Einstein, have recognized the need to separate morality from religion. Few thinkers believe human morality is absolute and divinely inspired. Jefferson believed all religious teaching should be eliminated in the public school system and that it should be replaced with moral teachings. We can obtain some agreement on human morality whereas we will never get agreement on god's morality. Einstein said, "In their struggle for the ethical good, teachers must have the stature to give up the personal God."

Morality differs in each social group. The moral code of the cannibal is different from one that doesn't condone eating human flesh. The moral code of a society that practices polygamy is different from one that does not. As the world shrinks, the morality of mankind tends to become a morality for all.

When India was under British rule, Indian morality allowed the placing of the surviving wife on the funeral pyre of her deceased husband so that both would be together in the afterlife. In the South, it was perfectly acceptable to prevent blacks from participating in elections and lynching them for real or imaginary violations of the social code. All white juries exonerated white defendants for their crimes against blacks. In Mississippi, one white juror was reported to have said that they could have rendered their not guilty verdict sooner but for the fact that they had to stop for a soda. In this case, the exonerated defendants sold their story to a magazine, cheerfully confessing their crime.

Morality between and among social groups varies greatly, proving that morality is man-made, not god-made. The people in India stopped burning widows and the South was forced to give up segregation and Jim Crow laws. The majority would no longer support such barbaric practices.

This country along with others is now in the process of trying to change the immoral custom of killing innocent women, men, and children as a means to achieve a political end. The efforts to combat terrorism in peace and collateral damage in war must be pursued. Hopefully we will succeed, but it will be a long worldwide struggle.

Conclusion:

Many believe that religion causes people to be moral, but the goodness of man does not depend upon god, nor is the fear of god adequate to the situation. The individual, who through thought, reasoning, and logic decides that he cannot believe in the god of Abraham is frequently more kind, more charitable, and thus more moral than many true believers. Most of our friends would remain as good as they are today if they never went to church again. Likewise, we see regular churchgoers who have no hesitation in engaging in lying and cheating. In fact, many scams against churchgoers are perpetrated by fellow churchmen. John Lovejoy Elliott wrote, "I have known many good men who believed in God. I have known many good men who did not believe in God. But I have never met a human being who was good who did not believe in man."

We must admit that much of human morality is the fear of being caught. It is fear of the consequences, fear of the police, fear of public opinion, and in some cases the fear of hell, as much as it is a desire to be good. For whatever reason, if it keeps your fist from my nose and your garbage out of my yard, I am for it. The problem with the fear of god is that the punishment is too far removed from the deed to be effective. If god does not punish man for evil until after he dies, man must assume that function. If god does not publicize and enforce its own moral code, then man must establish and enforce a moral code for humanity.

The moralities of religion are vague, poorly communicated, and do not convey their relative importance. We cannot determine how serious they are in god's eyes. We may believe that god does not approve of divorce, but how big a sin is it? Is divorce immoral? If marriages are made in heaven, why does god allow them to deteriorate? Does god's punishment vary with the importance of the sin? Are Hitler's sins treated with the same severity as a divorcee's sin?

The morality of religion and god is exemplified by the story of the Catholic priest who met one of his parishioners who had not been to confession recently. The priest asked the fellow why he hadn't been to confession to atone for his sins.

The parishioner replied, "Father, why should I ask for forgiveness for my minor misdeeds and sins when God commits acts of such enormous criminality. He takes husbands from wives, wives from husbands, and babies from mothers. It is not I but God who is the sinner."

As a poet has written, "God forgive my little sins on thee, and I'll forgive your big ones on me."

Most religions spend too much time on sin and not enough on human morality. There should not be a Buddhist, Jewish, Christian, or Muslim morality, only a humane human one. Religion has not civilized man; man must civilize religion.

According to some religious experts, being a person of good deeds and being moral, kind, and charitable still will not allow you an entrance into their heaven. Only by adoring and worshiping their deity is entrance allowed. This pernicious belief is an obstacle to a moral society. To believe that one can get into heaven only by accepting a belief in a specific prophet or god, no matter how moral, kind, or charitable one has been, is absurd as well as detrimental to human society.

To convince themselves and others that god is present and active in their lives, believers give god credit for man's morality, to the detriment of humankind. Furthermore, blaming satan for man's evil detracts from the moral responsibility of humanity.

Pascal wrote, "Let us, therefore, strive to think clearly; for such is the principle of morality."

What is morality in any given time or place? It is what the majority then and there happen to like and immorality is what they dislike.

Alfred North Whitehead

GUILT AND FEAR

Guilt and fear are two powerful weapons wielded by religion. Guilt is the feeling that we have done something wrong or violated some rule or protocol. Fear, on the other hand, is an anxiety or a feeling of dread. We feel guilty when we realize that we have hurt our loved one's feelings. We are afraid of going into a dark alley, face an angry supervisor at work, or face our parents when we are bringing home an awful report card. We are afraid of the unknown as well as the consequences of something we haven't done right. We are afraid of being caught and punished for breaking a law or a commandment.

Guilt:

Guilt is a function of man's higher brainpower and results from doing something or thinking something that is considered wrong. Man appears to be the only member of the animal kingdom who experiences guilt. According to Mark Twain, "Man is the only member of the animal kingdom who blushes and needs to."

The guilt created when one does something wrong is called conscience, which serves us well. It is our conscience that makes us think about what we did and the consequence of our actions. Most of us would not steal from a store even if we knew that no one was watching. We know that such an act is wrong and we must live with that knowledge.

On the other hand, one may feel guilty when one does something he has been taught is wrong even if that teaching is questionable, inconsequential, or untrue. Religion is full of inconsequential guilt-producing beliefs. Examples of these beliefs are going to church on the Sabbath; saying prayers every night; getting circumcised if one is male; having holy water sprinkled on one's head; going to confession; fasting; praying five times a day; making signs of the cross; abstaining from certain foods such as pork or beef; or any of the hundreds of beliefs perpetrated by the priests, preachers, rabbis, and others. We can legitimately question whether an all-powerful god, the creator of the universe, would be interested in tracking such inconsequential actions and for what purpose. The guilt that religions create over minor inconsequential human behavior is a drain on the human psyche. It psychologically paralyzes many believers. Often believers do not distinguish between the important things we should feel guilty about and the inconsequential things about which nobody, not even god, should care about.

Fear:

Fear is another powerful tool employed by religion. The fear of hell, the fear of god, and the fear of the unknown are the weapons of choice of the religious establishment.

Fear of hell:

Halloween, whose roots go to pagan celebrations, is a harmless festival of make-believe dress-up for young children. Children wear imaginative costumes such as skeletons, witches, and goblins, and go from door to door in their neighborhoods collecting candy. Some organizations create haunted houses to frighten the children. Everyone knows that these haunted houses are not real and are just make-believe. Children usually have fun on Halloween. They do not know the difference between pagan and Christian holidays; they just know how to have fun.

Some fundamentalist churches, unhappy at the sight of children happily celebrating an allegedly pagan holiday, came up with an alternative to Halloween. A local church created a Christian "haunted house". The church staged a frightening exhibit for children and parents that depicted the horrors of hell. It showed what happens to children who die without accepting Jesus into their lives as compared to those who do. Hundreds of parents, in all seriousness, took their children through that frightening horror exhibit. The church then had the effrontery to say that it didn't want to scare the children and the adults, it merely wanted to let people know what hell was going to be like if they didn't accept Christ. Unfortunately, it is a sadistic act on the part of the church; on the other hand, if it is true, it is a sadistic act on the part of god.

Fear can be a powerful emotion. It ranges from simple apprehension to panic. As we evaluate the fear of hell and the hope of heaven, we find little proof of their existence. Preachers, to overcome the absence of discernible evidence, resort to hysterics and fear. Perhaps we should say as Galileo did, "I know it not" and pay attention to our present life, not our afterlife. Surely life is not simply an entrance exam for heaven with god grading all of the papers.

Fear of god:

It is not possible to love those you fear. You may respect them, pay homage to them, even agree with them, but the fear will always keep you wary and on edge. If god is love, it has a mighty peculiar way of expressing it. As one wag said, "He births ye – he weakens ye – and then he kills ye." The early Jews were so afraid of god that they would not write or say its name aloud. Their god was always "smiting" people. The fundamentalist's god has not shown much improvement.

This author remembers when he was a child, probably right after a Sunday sermon, telling his mother that he thought god had a lot more to answer for than he did. The reader can imagine the shock that statement generated. That comment, even by a sassy, mouthy kid can never be allowed. Fear means you cannot be playful with god or probe or question the passed-down beliefs about god.

Children used to be taught, "One stroke of his almighty rod can send young sinners quick to hell." That belief and fear is still being taught in one form or another.

If god gives man unconditional love, none need worry or fear an afterlife. If god gives unconditional love, there was and is no need for Jesus. Surely god did not need to kill Jesus to convince mankind of its mercy and love.

The Bible says, "The fear of the Lord is the beginning of wisdom." In reality, the fear of god is the beginning of guilt and an opening for manipulation by those who claim to speak for god. Many people never get over their fear of god or their fear of hell, no matter what their logic and reasoning tell them as they mature.

Throughout history fear has played a significant role in the affairs of mankind. Mel Gibson, a practicing Catholic, recently said that he stuck by his faith because, "I'm too scared of getting a bolt of lightning up my posterior." That fear perpetuated by religion in childhood continues into adulthood. Many have been made so fearful of god that they cannot think about it objectively. In fact, they will not even talk about god except to those who have similar beliefs.

Fear of the unknown:
We all face the fear of the unknown. We are afraid when we take a new job because we don't know what to expect in terms of collegiality, friendships, and workloads. Many are afraid of the dark because some danger

might be lurking there. Thomas Hobbes in 1651 in *Leviathan* wrote, "Fear of things invisible is the natural seed of religion." Religion plays on the fears of the unknown—death, heaven, hell, satan, demons, and on and on. A belief in demons, for example, was prevalent in the ancient world just as a belief in satan is prevalent today. St. Augustine in the 5th century believed demons had sex with women that resulted in the birth of witches. Many Christian religious leaders promote and sustain the fear of the antichrist. The antichrist is someone everybody loathes and every generation of faithful seems to discover a new one.

Conclusion:

In dealing with fears and guilts, the problem is differentiating those we should keep from those we should shed. The fear that if you keep on smoking you will develop emphysema or cancer of the lung is a legitimate fear based upon verifiable knowledge. The knowledge that if you play with fire you will be burned is based on experience.

On the other hand, fear and guilt based upon faith that has not been proven can scar you for life. The guilt, not to mention the fear of eternal retribution that is caused by not going to church, not saying your prayers, not being baptized, not insisting that your children go to Sunday school, can be overwhelming. When you are so filled with fear, you can not ask the obvious, "Why does an all-powerful god need constant praise and adoration?"

But the worst form of fear and guilt occurs when one is afraid to even think about such ideas as presented in this book. Many preachers would have us believe that we are headed straight to hell when we even question what they preach. The many concepts of god as presented by the various religions do not make sense. We should be able and allowed to observe the world and come to our own conclusions. We should not be slaves to the Bible or some other scripture. We have the right, neigh the responsibility, to think on our own terms. God should not be afraid of our using our brain and the knowledge, which has evolved over millions of years. Fear and guilt prevent us from challenging the orthodoxy, prevent us from overthrowing oppressive systems and beliefs, and prevent us from seeking alternatives to bankrupt, fear-mongering sermons from the pulpits.

If fear always deterred wrongdoing, it would be an efficient way to control human appetites, whether for food, sex, tobacco, alcohol, or drugs. Such is not the case. Fear does not always deter wrongdoing and punishment far from the wrongdoing is even less likely to deter it.

One should never underestimate the fear factor in human behavior but one should remember, the things one fears are never as bad as one can imagine. FDR was right, "The only thing we have to fear is fear itself."

Many do not fear god but all must fear what man does in the name of god.

Fear is the most destructive force in the world today. It is much easier to frighten people, and more profitable, than to persuade them.

Walter L. Stone

No passion so effectually robs the mind of all its powers of acting and reasoning as fear.

Edmund Burke

FREE WILL OR FATE

The concepts of free will and fate have been of interest to philosophers and theologians for generations. Free will is the ability to choose between alternatives on our own accord. Fate is the inevitability of a course of events beyond our control. As we ponder on free will and fate, we realize that it is an issue that cannot be solved with our present knowledge. We are the result of our genes, our environment, our education, and our experiences in life. But how much free will we have and how much we are constrained by the above factors is impossible to determine. As someone has said, life is like a boat in a great river with a strong current. You can sometimes steer your boat around the snags and shoals but the current will carry you where it will.

What is random and unpredictable and what is purposeful in nature cannot be determined; we do not know the cause or the purpose of the universe; we cannot even know if there is a cause or purpose for the universe.

It is impossible to determine the true extent of our free will. No one prepared a map for us and no one has given us a destination. We choose our own path and give meaning to our own lives. The meaning of our life is what we make of it and that meaning comes from within, not from an outside source.

The concept of fate enters into this discussion, as one has no control over fate, luck, karma, or destiny. We sorely need the serenity prayer, "God grant me the serenity to accept the things I cannot change, the courage to change the things I can and the wisdom to know the difference." One may have the free will to buy a lottery ticket but it is the luck of the draw that lets one win. It is fate that you were born of parents in a specific place and at a specific time. We must accept many things that occur in our lives on fate. Our birth, genes, surroundings, and IQ are all matters of fate. Freedom of the will may be more limited than we like to think and the luck of the draw may play a larger role than we care to admit.

It is obvious that all of us are the result of our genes and our environment. It is impossible to know what the mix is. The frightening thing about parenthood is that we as parents are responsible for both the genes and the environment of our children.

Those who are blessed with good genes, good parents, and encouraged to read and study, should have empathy for those who are not so fortunate. Choices are limited without those lucky circumstances over which we had little or no control. Individuals with mental deficiencies, psychiatric illnesses, Alzheimer's disease, diabetes or other diseases, do not have the freedom of those without such handicaps. Those who were born in a society where food is scarce, poverty is rampant, and opportunities are limited, do not have the freedoms of those born in a free and prosperous society. Those who were taught to think dogmatically in childhood have limited freedom to think rationally in adulthood compared to those who were raised in an atmosphere of openness and allowed, even encouraged, to think for themselves.

Life is a multivariate system; we can control some variables but not all. We may be able to anticipate some events based upon our knowledge of how these variables interact, but not all of them. We know that when we leave for work in the morning we have a reasonable chance of arriving at our office; but we cannot predict and can never know when a drunk driver will crash into us. We can never know or predict an automobile accident nor can we predict many of the other calamities of life. We are reasonably sure that we will have a good time when we go to a concert but we cannot predict an accidental fire in the concert hall. There are many times when our free will is constrained as it meets with the free will of others or meets the unexpected consequences of the natural world.

The fact that we are victims of fate or of unexpected events as noted above, does not allow us to blame others for our actions. It is easy to blame parents, teachers, employers, or others, but we must finally accept responsibility for ourselves. We gain maturity when we learn the limitations of our free will and the role of random events in our lives. When we learn that, we can stop blaming others and learn to assume responsibility for the actions that are under our control. The sooner we learn that our actions have consequences, the better off we will be. Man's first commandment should be emphasized:

YOU ARE RESPONSIBLE
FOR YOUR OWN ACTIONS

This commandment is absolutely necessary for our mental well being as well as for social order. You frequently hear, "It's in god's hands now," as people realize they have done all they can to solve a problem. Some believe in a god who controls and micromanages their life but most realize that they have done everything they could to solve the problem and beyond that there is nothing to gain by worrying about it. They simply accept their fate, which they cannot control.

We may not like the fact that random and accidental events determine our lives but that does not alter the reality of it. As we observe the unpredictability of life, we should realize that an intelligent, all-powerful, divine being does not control it.

To deny the freedom of the will is to make morality impossible.

J.A. Froude

GOOD AND EVIL

If you thought freedom of the will vs. fate was difficult, good and evil are even more of an enigma. Although we think we know the difference between good and evil, we have all seen bad things turn out to be good and good things that turn out to be bad.

If you were to win a large lottery, that's good. Right? Not necessarily. The money could cause bickering in the family, loss of privacy, harassment from strangers, divorce, jealousy, and hatred – even murder. Thus, what started out to be a good and fortunate event turns out to be bad. Sometimes, when something bad happens in our lives, it may end up changing our lives for the better. For example, some one who is laid off or fired may decide to take stock of his or her life and do something more meaningful. A person who stutters may overcome that problem to become a great orator. Thus, something that started out to be bad ends up being good for the individual as well as for society. It seems good and evil can best be judged on hindsight.

The old saying, "Be careful what you wish for, you may get it" reveals how good can become bad and bad can become good and the difficulty distinguishing good from evil. When good and evil are so intermingled, it may be impossible to tell them apart at any one time.

The concept of good and evil becomes even more complicated when applied to god. Believers maintain that god is good. They also maintain that only god is capable of creation; only god could create the cosmos and all that is in it; only god could create small pox, anthrax, and AIDS; only god created the angels, including satan; only god creates floods, hurricanes, tornadoes, and erupting volcanoes; and only god could create hell with its fiery furnace.

Extending this logic, it is obvious that only god could create evil. Thus, logically speaking, god is both evil and good. Heaven forbid! By definition and fiat, man created a perfect, good, and righteous god. Now it turns out that god is evil too! Some maintain that god's goodness is different from man's goodness, but that does not excuse cruelty and hatred by god or religion.

Theoretically, we should know the difference between good and evil. Only psychopaths, it is said, don't know the difference. But research shows that even philosophers have difficulty with good and evil. Theologians and clergy who are supposed to know the difference are also in the same quandary. Theologians say that god is good but admit that it was god who created satan.

Then they turn around and put the burden of fighting satan and evil on humans! It should be obvious that good and evil are man made concepts and that we cannot judge them by a god who works in mysterious ways. Good and evil, as is morality, are determined by man for the benefit of man's well being.

All we can make of this mess of good and evil is that we should be slow to judge the actions of other people. Many of us find ourselves in the position of St. Augustine with his oft quoted prayer, "Please God make me pure; but not yet." There is a saying that there is so much good in the worst of us and so much bad in the best of us that we should be slow to judge. There is another saying, "What you are speaks so loudly that I cannot hear what you are saying." We must be careful judging the motives of others. Few people have a clear insight into their own motives, let alone understanding others' motives.

Most Americans agree that the tragedy of 9-11-01 was evil. However, out of this tragedy came kindness, empathy, patriotism, dedication, heroism, and a common goal. But it did not come out of nowhere. The Taliban of Afghanistan who was behind the dastardly act was trained and equipped by the west to fight the communists. After the fall of the communist regime in Afghanistan, somebody should have kept an eye on them.

DeFoe, in *Robinson Crusoe,* wrote about cannibalism and discussed the problem of good and evil as follows:

According to their dreadful customs, being all cannibals, they would kill and eat them... But I began, with cooler and calmer thoughts, to consider what I was going to engage in; what authority or call had I to pretend to be judge and executioner upon these men as criminals, whom Heaven had thought fit, for so many ages, to suffer unpunished? .... How do I know what God himself judges in this particular case? It is certain these people do not commit this as a crime; it is not against their own consciences reproving or their lights reproaching them.

Perhaps cannibalism is god's way of solving the food shortage and the population explosion in one fell swoop. On the other hand, since you and I might be the ones eaten, we'd best label it evil and make sure god agrees with us.

Those who maintain absolute standards of good and evil, as well as absolute standards of right and wrong, are dangerous. They cannot see the many shades of gray between black and white. They are unable to understand the many nuances of life in general and of morality in particular. Those who maintain absolute standards in the name of god are doubly dangerous. Like the paranoid schizophrenic who hears voices, they hear the voice of god who may tell them to do despicable things.

By common definition, god is good. The devil is evil. One must feel sorry for the devil. He gets the blame, not only for man's evil ways, but also for god's dirty work. As yet, satan hasn't been blamed for natural disasters but he gets credit for the rest of evil. Obviously, the devil did not create itself – god was responsible for that. An all-powerful, all-knowing being must be credited for evil just as it is given credit for everything else.

Despite the difficulty in defining good and evil there are some commonly accepted concepts of good and evil. Man has a duty to resist evil even though god seems to be reluctant to deal with it in our lifetime.

No one believes that life is fair but few blame the maker of that life for its unfairness. Who else could be responsible for it? The clergy would have you believe that everything is going to come out roses after you die but only if you accept their beliefs. Wanna bet? Death will be fair to all only if you believe as the nonbelievers do – when you're dead, you're dead.

St. Augustine maintained that the existence of god could be proved by the existence of evil. In reality, the existence of evil proves there is no perfect divine being in charge.

The man who lives by the Golden Rule today never has to apologize for his actions tomorrow.
Anonymous

FANTASY

Fantasy, although it is frequently looked down upon and discouraged, serves us well. We all grew up on wonderful children's stories and Arthurian legends of bravery, heroism, and virtue. Fantasy gives us magnificent literature. We still love *Alice in Wonderland*. Science fiction is imagination allowed to run wild into the future. Authors such as J. R. R. Tolkien and C. S. Lewis spun fantastic tales. We enjoy *Star Wars* movies. Kids for generations loved cowboy movies where virtuous cowboys stand up against corrupt and evil thugs and win. We love Disneyland, a land of fantasy. Our lives are enriched by fantasies.

Fantasies make our lives more pleasant. Even when we are faced with difficult circumstances in life, there is nothing to stop us from taking a book and retreating into a world of fantasy. Fantasy helps us, at least for a short time, escape from the harsh realities of life. It helps us maintain our sanity.

Problems arise when people confuse fantasy with reality. It is one thing to fantasize what you would do if you won a multimillion dollar lottery; it is quite another to start spending money based on that fantasy.

There comes a time in our life when we realize that Santa Claus is not real; the story is made-up. It is one of the lessons we learn early in life—we learn to distinguish fantasy from reality. We may fantasize about winning lotteries but most of us are sane enough not to waste our money on that fantasy. When fantasy becomes confused with reality, it is called delusion. One person's delusion is another person's religion.

It is disheartening to watch grown men and women confuse fantasy and reality. It is amazing to watch people pine away for Jesus, who has been dead for over two thousand years, as they tell one another that he will come back to earth and take them to heaven. It is not pleasant to hear religious people say that god loves us out of one side of their mouth and that god will punish us out of the other. If god loves all, why is hell necessary? Some cannot distinguish their enemies from the enemies of god.

Some fantasies have strange consequences. Jesus reportedly threw the moneylenders out of the temple. Wonderful story. However, our commerce and society is dependent on moneylenders—we call them banks. One cannot run a business without someone lending money to keep the business going. Some Islamic nations ban interest on loans—but the moneylenders and interest did not go away; they simply called it something else. Confusion between fantasy and reality creates a warped world.

We should keep the fantasies that make us feel better or make our life more tolerable. This is true for the fantasies of god, heaven, sex, and eternal life. To act upon those fantasies as if they were true is dangerous, not only for us as individuals, but also for others. Enjoy your fantasies; just realize what they are.

There is a story of a little boy, who like most other boys, had his good days and his bad days. When asked if he knew why, he answered, "When I am happy I push my thoughts around. When I am sad my thoughts push me around." Fantasy may help you push your thoughts around. If so, go for it but don't accept others' fantasies. They are just thoughts that will push you around.

Truth can be cruel. Fantasy, illusion, and delusion can be comforting. It is easy to be fooled by your wish to believe – whether it is in immortality, heaven, or an angel looking out for your interests. Wishful thinking may bring comfort but it doesn't bring truth or reality. "Coulda, woulda, shoulda" are fantasies.

Today most of us consider witches to be a fantasy, but they were not a fantasy in the past nor today for some. Theologian Meric Casaubon in 1668 reasoned in *Of Credulity and Incredulity* that witches must exist because everyone believes in them. Today theologians use that same logic to prove there is a god –

since so many people believe in god, there must be one.

John Wesley, the founder of Methodism, said, "The giving up of witches is in effect the giving up of the Bible." William Blackstone in his *Commentaries on the Laws of England* in 1765 wrote, "To deny the possibilities, nay, actual existence of witchcraft and sorcery is at once flatly to contradict the revealed word of God in various passages of both the Old and New Testament." The Bible proclaims, "Thou shalt not suffer a witch to live."

Use fantasy for your own satisfaction. Create your own god. Most have done that. There may only be 9,900 religions in the world today but there are millions of gods, all created by individuals who create their own. Let's use a little fantasy here. What would the world be like if those ancient Jews had decided to go with Astarte, the female goddess in vogue in the Middle East at that time, instead of Yahweh? Just think, instead of a cruel masculine god we might now have a maternal, unconditional loving goddess.

If a woman remarries after her husband dies, who does she join in heaven? Is there any sex there? Just fantasize your sex afterlife. Most do. Fantasize heaven. Heaven is whatever you want it to be. If you like dogs and cats, they will be there. Your friends and parents will be at the age you most enjoyed and remembered them. If you are into food there will be gourmet buffets. If you are lusting for sex, you can have 72 virgins attend to your desires. Don't forget though, your heaven may be the virgins' hell and the dogs and cats may have fleas.

Many fantasize that they will be with their loved ones after they die. But what if your parents' heaven is in their youth, before you were born? What then? Certainly their heaven won't be as they were when they died – blind, deaf, senile, and demented.

Then there is the fantasy of hell, so terrible as to scare men, women, and children. Eternal burning and damnation. For what? Not for being bad or evil but for refusing to pay homage to god. What really seems to make god and its believers angry is to deny god's very existence.

The myths and fantasies of heaven do little harm until people do injury to others to get there. The myths and fantasies of hell with its painful eternity do great harm. Religions persist because people want to continue their fantasy of a heaven for themselves and their loved ones and a hell for their enemies.

We have to allow others to believe what they want, but we should not allow them to undertake actions that are inimical to the public good based on their fantasies. It may be impossible to prevent a person from believing he will go to heaven if he kills an infidel, but he has no right to murder or instruct others to carry out that belief.

Reality can be so overwhelming that life needs to be spiced up with fantasy from time to time, but fantasies should be private and shared only in select situations.

It is all right to build castles in the air provided we put foundations under them.

Henry Thoreau

SKEPTICISM

Skeptics do not enjoy the best of reputations but their attitude of questioning and probing and their unwillingness to accept things on faith serves us well. Skepticism is the questioning of all beliefs. Even well established truths can be questioned and frequently can be shown to be wanting. Einstein's theory of relativity turned the comfortably established Newtonian physics upside down. Darwin started a conceptual revolution with his theory of evolution that shook the foundations of Judaism and Christianity. Despite virulent attacks against evolution, it is here to stay and the religious believers have no choice but to accommodate to Darwin's theories. Even religion benefits from the unbelievers. Martin Luther questioned certain beliefs and practices of the Catholic Church and started the Protestant movement. Over two thousand five hundred years ago Buddha expressed his skepticism about gods. The religion that bears his name is the only major religion that maintains a studied neutrality about the issue of gods.

Skepticism is the effective use of our ability to reason, evaluate, and come to conclusions based on evidence. Skeptics do not accept something solely based on belief or authority. While religion maintains that the various scriptures are revealed to humans by god, skeptics remain doubtful if not actively hostile to such claims of authority.

We all should develop a healthy dose of skepticism in everything that has not been proven and especially in matters of faith and assumptions, be they expressed or hidden. As noted above, one must even be skeptical of those ideas that have been proven. For instance, physicists accepted Einstein's idea that the velocity of light was constant. However, there are upstart physicists who think that, at the time the universe began, that assumption was not true.

Some people claim that skeptics are arrogant. Some may be. In point of fact, skeptics, because they make a conscious and difficult effort to swim against the current, are often humble, self-effacing people. Most skeptics recognize better than others the limitations of their knowledge and are eager to learn more. It is the true believer, with his absolute certainty, who is arrogant. When Bertrand Russell, a skeptic, was asked, "Will you die for your beliefs?" He was reported to have replied, "Of course not. I could be wrong."

Skeptics see things in shades of gray. Dogmatic believers see only in black and white. Skeptics hold their views tentatively and change them, as more evidence is available.

They do not resist change. Believers do not waste time on questioning their assumptions or examining the foundations of their knowledge and beliefs. They live on faith and dogma. The skeptic realizes that what you think you know may turn out to be wrong. The true believer cannot allow himself to believe he could be wrong. The skeptic says, "Show me." The believer says, "Don't confuse me with facts; my mind is made up."

President Jimmy Carter described fundamentalism in this way:

> Fundamentalism means the thinker is absolutely sure he is right. You don't want to learn new facts, because they might disturb your previous opinions. You become convinced that your truths have come from God and anyone who disagrees with you is wrong, and the next step is that they're inferior and the ultimate case is, they're subhuman. That leads to a lot of persecution in the world.

Chet Raymo in *Skeptics and True Believers* and Carl Sagan in *The Demon-Haunted World* do a magnificent job of pointing out the many beliefs that men and women insist on holding even after irrefutable evidence against them. Examples of a few such beliefs follow:

Millions of people start their day reading astrology columns in daily newspapers. As a rough assumption, about twenty million

Americans share each astrological sign. These twenty million Americans include babies, children in school, young adults, adults, senior citizens, and seriously ill and disabled. But the astrology column for one of the signs says, "Romantic relation heats up." Is it really possible that the romantic life of 20 million Scorpios heats up on cue? If one probes further, astrological predictions are vague statements such as: dealing with banks may prove frustrating; remember diet; exercise resolutions; work hard to attain objectives. It may tell Geminis to leave early for an appointment and Cancers that domestic order is lacking.

Probing still further, one will notice that these predictions contain a set of phrases that repeat themselves all through the signs. One can easily compile a list of these statements, just write a simple program that randomly assigns them to various signs and there you have – an astrology column! Of course, logic and analysis of evidence have no bearing on the belief in astrology. Most people know that they are just plain junk but they keep reading them anyway.

In addition to astrology, Tarot cards, psychics, and spiritualists continue to influence many people. One can, for instance, consult with psychics on the telephone. Without seeing you or knowing anything about you, they can tell your future. These psychics are frauds. They keep the callers on long-distance phone lines as long as possible and many of them skirt the laws of the United States by diverting the phone calls to overseas telephone lines. Without claiming to be psychics, we can predict with absolute certainty that if you make a call to a telephone consultant, your telephone bill will be huge!

Many people continue to believe in unidentified flying objects (UFOs). There is a cult whose founder claims to have been abducted by aliens and he walks around wearing a space suit. This sect came into prominence recently by claiming that they cloned humans. There are numerous books on UFOs and Roswell, New Mexico is the Mecca for UFO believers.

There are obviously many unidentified objects in the sky—unidentified airplanes, weird climatic phenomena, meteors, and debris from artificial satellites and spacecraft. However, the belief that little green men are taking women aboard their space ship for sex deserves skepticism. The Air Force, after an intense lobbying of UFO believers, spent millions of dollars studying UFOs and found no evidence that aliens from a distant planet had visited earth. Of course, the believers would not accept such studies—they see conspiracies everywhere; for example, the United States is hiding the truth. Certainly skeptics must keep an open mind on whether there is life elsewhere in the universe, but they will await further evidence of such life.

The Shroud of Turin was scientifically proven to have originated in the middle ages and therefore cannot be the shroud of Jesus. The shroud is a fraud perpetrated on believers, but that evidence has had little effect on the believers and their veneration for that piece of cloth.

In Colombia, South America it was predicted that on June 6, 1966 (666 is the biblical number of the beast) the antichrist was going to claim any soul who had not been baptized. You can imagine the effects of that prediction on the devout. It certainly increased baptisms.

But the extent of dubious beliefs is much more widespread. Literally millions believe in angels, heaven, hell, miracles, and reincarnation. Over eleven million people have purchased the *Prayer of Jabez*. Folks want to believe that if they pray, praise god, have faith, and tithe, god will bless them with wealth, health, and all sorts of goodies. But nothing fails like prayer.

Countless millions believe in the power of prayer but there is no evidence that prayer has any effect on anything or anybody except the individual doing the praying. It may be of some benefit psychologically to the individual praying, and even lighten the burden of life, but the benefits are imaginary and short-lived. Praying is like talking to a deaf, mute, invisible psychiatrist. Prayer can be an expression of gratitude for the good things in one's life but usually it is just a big "gimme"—god gimme this and god gimme that. It is a gimme for eternal bliss with all of your loved ones around you. Prayers are wishes thrown up to the sky. There is no harm in prayers as long as you work like hell to make your wishes come true. However, others should not be expected to stand by quietly and reverently as you throw your wishes up in the air.

James H. Leuba, a Bryn Mawr psychologist, conducted a survey to determine how many educated people believed in god. He found that only 43.9% of physical scientists, 30.5% of biologists, 24.2% of psychologists, 46.3% of sociologists, and 48.3% of historians believed in god. The philosophers submitted such vague answers that the results could not be tabulated. Leuba also noted that a college education resulted in lessening religious beliefs. So, if you want your children to grow up to be religious bigots, don't let them go to college.

Most people do not critically examine their religious beliefs. They do not want to expose their god to logic and reasoning, as they know their beliefs cannot stand scrutiny. Without such scrutiny, religions are allowed to express ridiculous, even harmful views, without criticism and challenge.

Francis Bacon in 1620 wrote, "What a man would like to be true, he preferentially believes." T.H. Huxley in his *Credo* wrote, "To think wishfully, to rest in comfortable illusion..." Bertrand Russell pointed out in *On God and Reason:*

> We hold our beliefs because to give them up makes us unhappy. We have had those statements repeated so many times since infancy that we cannot give them up. Even those superstitions we

know to be false may give us a
sense of dis-ease, such as breaking
a mirror or having a black cat cross
our path.

The discomfort and pain that results in
giving up a belief inculcated in childhood can
be overwhelming. Many cannot and will not
give up those beliefs. The faith that is inculcated
from childhood can be comfortable because the
believers are provided with a neat set of beliefs
where everything is explained and put in its
place, but it will only be comfortable if one does
not question it. It is much easier to keep
believing that pagans are your enemies and
should be destroyed rather than saying, "Wait
a minute, some of our beliefs are as inane as
theirs, and like theirs, some of our beliefs are
just myths."

It is not religion that makes us consider
issues such as the meaning of life, good and
evil, and life after death. It is our innate
curiosity to ponder those questions—those
questions existed long before organized
religions were established and they continue,
to haunt us. While religion deals with those
questions with mysticism and dogma, science
tries to answer them with objective observation
and critical thinking. Carl Sagan wrote in *The
Demon-Haunted World:*

Science has beauty, power, and
majesty that can provide spiritual
as well as practical fulfillment. But
superstition and pseudo-science
keep getting in the way, providing

easy answers, casually pressing our awe buttons, and cheapening the experience.

The many religions and their diverse beliefs give the skeptic much to question. There are thousands of gods and goddesses in the history of mankind. The believer insists there is only one god—his. He asserts that he knows god, but in the next breath he maintains that god is incomprehensible and works in mysterious ways. Some go to the extent of claiming that they talk to god every day. If one were to collect the directives god gives to believers and analyze them, they would be very similar to astrological predictions—sometimes they are true, but usually they are not.

The believer insists that god loves you. The skeptic then asks why god created hell. The believer will say god doesn't give a person more problems than he can handle. The skeptic says baloney – why do you think people commit suicide? The believer says faith can move mountains. The skeptic says show me a mountain moved by faith. The believer says god is responsible for life. The skeptic says then it should take better care of it. The believer says the prince of peace will come. The skeptic says that after 2000 years you might have reason to wonder. The believer sees and hears what he wants to see and hear. The skeptic says prove it. The skeptic's experience tells him the cosmos does not really care about man's fate – only man cares about man's fate. The believer thinks god cares greatly about man's fate and his own personal fate in particular.

The skeptic notes that god doesn't show any more concern for humans than it does for the rest of the biological and physical world.

Women and men are united by their doubts; they are separated by their convictions. It is wise to be a skeptic. It is up to the believer to prove his suppositions. Moses proclaimed an eye for an eye and a tooth for a tooth—an unlimited vengeance that makes us blind and toothless. Jesus softened this vengeful statement by advising us to turn the other cheek. This was an improvement but unreasonable and never seriously practiced. Even Christian nations maintain huge armies and weapons of mass destruction. Now we need another prophet to come along and proclaim, "Punishment according to the deed."

Isaac Asimov wrote, "Inspect every piece of pseudoscience and you will find a security blanket, a thumb to suck, a skirt to hold." There can be no objection to sucking your thumb, hanging on to your blanket, or even holding on to your mother's skirt; but you should not be allowed to smother others with your "blankie".

What we see depends mainly on what we look for.
                                          John Lubbock

You sometimes see a lot just by looking.
                                          Yogi Berra

Can God make a rock so heavy he can't lift it?
                                          A young skeptic

THINK - THINK - THINK

What advice should we give to a group of high school, college, or university students embarking upon their education? We should tell them to think - think - think - reason - reason - reason. We should tell them that the purpose of their education, as opposed to passed down or revealed dogmatic religious or political belief systems, is to constantly disturb and rearrange their cognitive frameworks and their belief systems.

Thinking involves identifying and challenging the assumptions behind your beliefs. Assumption is the taking for granted a belief without subjecting it to critical evaluation and proof. Remember the childhood saying, "Suppose one thing, suppose another, suppose a monkey was your brother." Although one must take many things for granted in life, one should always strive to critically examine information and search for truth and knowledge.

Years ago, one of my medical school

professors, in his opening lecture, wrote on the blackboard in large letters:

ASSUME

Then under this he wrote in bold letters:

ASS U ME

He read it aloud: Assume makes an ass out of you and me. I have never forgotten that simple but profound lesson. Nor should anyone seeking truth.

Thinkers are a nuisance. They are a pain in the butt as they are always questioning authority and asking why, when, how, who, and where, and searching for answers. They are always looking for verification of their beliefs and assumptions. Many people do not like their attitudes. George Bernard Shaw observed, "The power of accurate observation is commonly called cynicism by those who have not got it."

Thinking is difficult because you may have to change your opinions and your beliefs based on the available evidence. Ignorance, on the other hand, is quite comforting. Charles Darwin in *The Descent of Man* wrote, "Ignorance more frequently begets confidence than does knowledge: it is those who know little, and not those who know much, who so positively assert that this or that problem will never be solved by science." (Carl Sagan's *The Demon – Haunted World* presents an in depth treatise on thinking.)

People who think must keep an open mind and be receptive to other assumptions.

The dogmatist should remember Senator Everett Dirksen's words, "I always like to put sugar on my words, as I never know when I will have to eat them."

Descartes, in his *Meditations*, wrote:

It is some time since I first realized how many false opinions I accepted as true from my childhood, and how doubtful was the entire structure of thought which I had built upon them. I therefore understood that I must, if I wanted to establish anything at all in science that was firm and liable to last, once and for all rid myself of all the opinions I had adopted, and start from an entirely new foundation.

What we want to believe is not necessarily true just as what seems impossible to one person does not make it impossible to all. The shedding of prejudice is absolutely necessary to find truth.

Religion and Thinking: Religious dogmatists use a number of techniques to prevent their followers from engaging in independent thinking. These are: hope for everlasting life; inculcation of belief in an officially sanctioned dogma; raising the specter of eternal punishment to those whose thinking differs from the official dogma; and emphasis on tradition, ritual, and repetition. Other barriers to critical thinking include the mistaken ideas of causality, willful or inadvertent gullibility, and attempts to rationalize ones beliefs.

Hope: Most religions offer hope to their followers—most notably, hope for life after death. People who believe in a given deity, prophet, savior, or saint are assured that they will go to heaven as opposed to those who do not profess such faith.

Dogma: Each religion has its official dogma. The Apostles' Creed is the official dogma of many Christian churches:

> I believe in God, the Father Almighty, the Creator of heaven and earth, and in Jesus Christ, His only Son, our Lord: Who was conceived of the Holy Spirit, born of the Virgin Mary, suffered under Pontius Pilate, was crucified, died, and was buried. He descended into hell. The third day He arose again from the dead. He ascended into heaven and sits at the right hand of God the Father Almighty, whence he shall come to judge the living and the dead. I believe in the Holy Spirit, the holy catholic church, the communion of saints, the forgiveness of sins, the resurrection of the body, and life everlasting.

You will note there is nothing in the Apostles' Creed concerning living a good and moral life; only that you must believe the unbelievable and the unprovable to get to heaven. The Apostles' Creed pertains to words, not deeds. An ancient poet wrote, " A man of words and not of deeds, Is like a garden full of weeds."

Many Christian believers accept this creed—everything proclaimed in it. Adhering to the dogma is the one and only way to truth and heaven. Believing in anything else is false and may be subject to serious punishment. Other religious groups also have creeds, which they chant over and over. Believers are expected to memorize and repeat the dogmas and creeds until they become indelibly implanted in their minds.

Dogma differs from scientific theories. Scientific theories are open to challenge, revision, and determination that they are false. Doctrines are not subject to such challenge and examination. For example, there is no way to test or prove Jesus' divinity or to prove that he is the Son of God. In operational terms, we don't know what "Son of God" means. Does it mean that Jesus' genes were different from other humans? Does it mean that Jesus did not share genetic code with his mother? How exactly did god make Mary pregnant? If god has a supernatural way of creating a son, why did he create only one son? Why not more sons or daughters? We have no answers for such questions and we have no way to investigate them. There is no way to prove or disprove religious creeds. We cannot define Holy Ghost in operational terms and discover its properties. Does it have mass, shape, texture, color, etc.? We have to accept these terms on the basis of someone's assertions.

In contrast, science depends on skepticism. You must subject beliefs, theories, and assertions to examination. Every scientist's dream is to overthrow the prevailing theory and attach his or her name to a new one. Scientists face repeated failures in their search for truth. Einstein once remarked the best tool for a scientist is a wastebasket. Scientific theories are constantly changing and undergoing revisions. For instance, evolution is a scientific theory and is constantly being updated as the knowledge of nature increases. It is not an infallible, unchangeable, irrefutable belief like the dogma of god's creation.

While dogma dictates unquestioned obedience and discourages original thinking in our religious life, we are encouraged to do otherwise in our secular life i.e. to think for ourselves, to question authority, and persist in the quest for truth. Martin Luther's frightening statement, "Whoever wants to be a Christian must tear the eyes out of reason", reveals religion's reluctance to use reason and logic. But there are many who are unable to close their eyes to reason.

Punishment: Many churches convince their followers that if they doubt the veracity of their dogmas or their scriptures they will go to hell. Even worse, some religious bodies engage in inhumane punishments such as excommunication where family members are prohibited from having anything to do with the offending member. In some cases, the offenders may be killed. Descartes, for example, believed in reason over dogma but, to avoid a fight with the church, he continued to proclaim his belief in god. Galileo recanted his theory that the earth moves around the sun to avoid punishment. The Greek historian Polybius explains the role of fear in religion:

> Since the masses of the people are inconsistent, full of unruly desires, passionate and reckless of consequences, they must be filled with fears to keep them in order. The ancients did well, therefore, to invent gods, and the belief in punishment after death.

If religions used their fear and their gods to help maintain an orderly, humane society, then all might benefit whether the gods and the fears were true or not. But religions waste that fear to perpetuate their rituals, support their infrastructure, and maintain control over their believers. This defeats the abilities of religions to help maintain a peaceful and just society. In fact, the many religions cause rivalry, discord, and competition.

Tradition and rituals: Tradition and rituals that are inculcated from childhood act against independent thinking. The ritual of getting ready to go to church, wearing nice clothes, attending church, meeting and talking with friends, and going to lunch afterwards is comforting. Whether one liked to go to church in childhood or not, one always remembers fondly what a wonderful day Sunday was. In olden times, going to church was the only means of interacting with the community and Sundays were the only days when the entire family could be together, relax, and have a nice dinner. Even years later, many still recall mom's or grandma's cooking and can still smell the wonderful kitchen aromas. Rituals such as baptisms and coming of age festivals that occur in almost all religions are major milestones in people's lives. People regularly engage in traditions such as going on pilgrimages, visiting churches, temples, and mosques, attending revival meetings, and listening to priests and preachers as a way of maintaining and reinforcing their religious beliefs. Every year we see millions of Muslims trampling one another in a religious frenzy in Mecca, thousands of Jews at the Wailing Wall, and thousands paying homage to the Pope. All of these acts are remembered with fondness or reverence and are a way of making sure that the religious adherents remain loyal to their religious beliefs. If families would set aside one day a week for family activities instead of a Sabbath for god, society would benefit.

Causality: Another barrier to critical thinking is the mistaken association of cause and effect. People often confuse causality with correlation or juxtaposition. The fact that one thing follows another does not mean that the first thing caused the second thing. In terms of statistics, we call that relationship spurious. It is an accidental relationship and has no significant meaning. What we think is cause and effect may be nothing more than unexplained or accidental coincidences. The fact that a black cat crossed your path and you had a bad day does not mean that the black cat caused your bad day.   Simply because someone won a lottery or was cured of cancer does not mean that prayer caused it.   We need to remember that millions of people who prayed did not win the lottery and did not survive their cancer.   If two persons survived an accident where hundreds were killed, that doesn't mean that god chose those two people for special favor. Such an assertion begs the question,   "Why did god let hundreds perish and save just two?" If one examines superstitions and the beliefs on the efficacy of prayers, one will find that both fail more often than they succeed.   In any case, given this vast universe, there are countless events going on at the same time and they can easily be mistaken as cause and effect.

An interesting aspect of causality is the discussion as to whether religiosity causes mental illnesses.   For certain, there is a correlation between religion and psychoses, but whether religion causes mental illness is more difficult to establish.   Religious thoughts and beliefs, along with auditory and visual hallucinations, are an important aspect in many psychotic patients.   Religious efforts to make children believe the church dogma may eventually lead to their difficulty in distinguishing fantasy from reality when they become adults.   The indoctrination of religion may predispose the individual to illusions and delusions.   The many unprovable and impossible beliefs foisted upon the unsuspecting and naive mind can warp it permanently. The inability to discriminate between parables, metaphors, and reality may encourage the psychotic to "pluck out an eye" or "cut off a hand" if they "offend thee". The inability to tell the difference between the real and the unreal is a key element in psychoses. Some clinicians believe that a strict religious upbringing can be an important element in the development of depression, emotional disorders, and suicides. They also believe that it may cause a generally fearful response to life. The indoctrination of children with dogmatic unproven beliefs, without allowing them skeptical disbelief, is conducive to mental illness, guilt, fear, and anxiety as the child matures. A diet of fear and hate leads to neuroses and unhealthy obsessions.

On the other hand, if the religious believer can convince himself that god, Allah, Jesus, or angels are looking after his welfare, this may be an effective tranquilizer – thus causing less mental distress. Until this issue is studied, tested, and retested, we should keep an open mind. Perhaps Karl Marx was correct when he maintained that religion is the opiate of the masses but it is not the opiate of religion that harms humanity.

Gullibility: People are intentionally or unintentionally gullible. Gullibility is the failure to think critically. It is believing in someone or something without questioning. Scam artists and religious leaders prey on the gullible.

It is easier to reject overwhelming evidence than to give up your faith and admit that you are wrong. Preachers have a great way of blaming the victims. If your prayer does not cure you, you are simply not faithful enough – or they use the excuse that god works in mysterious ways. If the poisonous serpent kills you, you did not have enough faith. There is no way to counter that kind of logic.

Carl Sagan wrote of his amusement on seeing a cartoon of a fortune-teller reading his client's palm. The fortune-teller in all seriousness told the man, "You are very gullible." Though we all can be gullible from time to time, a little serious thinking could limit that gullibility. The number of believers in spirits, sorcery, astrology, UFOs, witches, faith healers, angels, even prayer, reinforces the fact that man is an irrational, feeling, emotional animal, as well as a rational, logical, thinking animal.

People are gullible for several reasons. They may simply want to please. They may be afraid to question or think. Gullibility is frequently based upon hope and desire. Advertisers as well as the clergy are very aware of this. One should repeat, "Fool me once, shame on you. Fool me twice, shame on me." Gullibility is being fooled repeatedly.

Rationalization: Søren Kierkegaard, the Danish philosopher and theologian, is much quoted by Christians. At the end of a long, incoherent discussion, he concluded that god exists just as he was taught in childhood. Kierkegaard couldn't prove this, so he maintained that one must accept Christianity based on faith alone. He coined the word fideism for the belief that truth can be based on faith. Kierkegaard's theory of fideism was his way of believing something that he could not prove with logic. His philosophy was a rationalization for his belief in Christianity. His premise that belief makes something true is patently untrue. People believe in many things that are not true. In fact, there are people who still believe the earth is flat. Kierkegaard was like C. S. Lewis, Philip Yancey, and other Christian apologists who are engaged in rationalizing their childhood beliefs. Nietzsche noted years ago, "A casual stroll through a lunatic asylum shows that faith does not prove anything."

Another example of rationalization is Pascal's wager, which says that it is better to believe and be wrong than to take a chance on not believing and be right. Pascal's wager is often used as justification for believing in an all-powerful, all-knowing god. Pascal wanted to be on safe ground just in case god existed and was as cruel as the clergy said it was.

The offer of hope; the teaching and memorization of dogma; the instilling of fear about life after death; the inculcating of the habit of rituals and traditions; the mistaken ideas of causality; the willful or inadvertent gullibility; and the attempts to rationalize one's beliefs – all work against critical thinking. It is much easier to believe and do the things our parents, grandparents, and others did, as we are familiar and comfortable with those traditions and rituals. Many choose not to risk their entrance into heaven and thus   follow whatever they were taught in childhood.

One should keep thinking, keep asking questions, and keep seeking answers. One should not be bamboozled by titles such as His Holiness, the Reverend, Archbishop, or whatever. We have access to wonderful library collections and instantaneous access to Internet resources. We should use them in searching for answers to questions that are answerable.

It is important to realize that all faiths, beliefs, assumptions, and truisms have varying degrees of proof and believability. In religion, you may be a believer, a believer in some things but not others, an agnostic, or a nonbeliever. So too can assumptions range from definite to unlikely. That is why we need to keep examining religious terminology and religious beliefs and subject them to further analysis. For instance, what do the terms   eternity and the will of god mean? Descartes advised us to study all of our beliefs and rank them in believability depending upon the amount and quality of the evidence for them. The certainty of our beliefs should be measured by the evidence we have. Francis Bacon insisted that all truths including religious truths be subjected to reason and logic.

One of the problems with truth is that it may be politically incorrect. Sometimes it is hard to accept truth. Philip Morris had to apologize to the public because one of its officials in the Czech Republic maintained that smoking decreased medical costs because people died prematurely and thus saved millions of medical dollars. The Czech official was right. When you add the large amount of taxes collected on tobacco to the shortened lifespan from smoking, you find that smoking actually saves society eighty-three cents per pack. But that conclusion is not something that most of us want to hear. Similarly, subjecting religious doctrines and beliefs to critical analysis may lead to startling and unpopular reactions. It is not socially acceptable to criticize anyone's god or religion, no matter how illogical, ridiculous, or harmful the belief. Respecting others who do not share our beliefs, be they political, academic, or religious, doesn't come easily.

So we should say to all who are starting on the road to learning: **Think – think – think. Reason – reason – reason.** The search for truth is a never-ending quest. Endeavor to see things as they are, not as they might or should be.

As soon as you can say what you think, and not what some other person has thought for you, you are on your way to being a remarkable man.

Sir James Barrie

For every generation there has to be some fool who will speak the truth as he sees it.

Boris Pasternak

The simple believes everything, but the prudent looks where he is going.

Proverbs 14: 15

LIFE IS A LABORATORY

L ife is a constant search for truth. Science is the technique for establishing truth. A scientist starts with an assumption or a hypothesis, designs a method or an experiment to verify that hypothesis, collects facts or data, then analyzes the data to see if they support the hypothesis. The hypothesis, based on the collected data, is either accepted or rejected. In some cases it may be determined that the results are inconclusive as the collected data neither support nor reject the hypothesis. In this instance, if the hypothesis is sufficiently important, further and more refined experiments will be conducted and the process of evaluating the hypothesis starts all over again.

A critical aspect of the scientific method is communication. Scientists communicate their experiments to their peers. Scientific peers read and evaluate the submitted manuscripts before publishing the findings in a peer-reviewed journal. Scientific publication is critical to the scientific method because, based on the details supplied in the published material, other scientists try to replicate those experiments and verify the work of the original research. The publication of experimental details in open literature and the independent verification of those experiments by other scientists is the backbone of the scientific method. The impact of science lies in its open communication where anyone can verify, challenge, and extend the original findings.

Science does not flourish in secrecy and scientific knowledge is not spread by non-replicable methods such as revelations from personal gods, witnessing of results, testimonials from people whose lives were allegedly changed, belief in the scientists' moral rectitude, nor in faith that cannot be verified. Scientists from time to time may engage in fraud or commit errors in designing the experiments and in collecting, analyzing, and interpreting the data. The open scientific communication acts as a check against fraud and error. For instance, a number of years ago, some scientists announced that they had achieved nuclear fusion at room temperatures and promised that their discoveries would lead to abundant cheap energy. No sooner had they announced their discovery than interested scientists tried to replicate their methods and failed to verify the occurrence of cold fusion.

The precautionary principle – the principle that dictates that you must prove something safe before you can develop it – will stop all development. One cannot test something before it is developed nor can one predict the future without testing. To eliminate all risk is to eliminate all innovation.

The scientific method allows us to test our assumptions, discard those that are false, and retain those that are confirmed by the data. Those confirmed hypotheses form the basis of our knowledge. The benefits of science and technology which we enjoy every day are the results of this scientific method.

Religion, by contrast, is not based on the scientific method. While scientific experiments, observations, and conclusions are open to challenge and revision, religion does not allow such challenges. In fact, to challenge religion is to be excluded from the group. Religions cannot tolerate people in their ranks who disagree with them.

Religion is based on non-replicable methods such as prayers, testimonials, revelations, and miracles. Unlike a carefully designed and conducted science experiment, a double blind, controlled study of prayer has never been conducted. If a prayer fails, we would not be able to draw reliable conclusions—as god may not have wanted to grant the prayer; the person who is praying may not be sufficiently virtuous and prayerful; the person praying may not have prayed sufficiently hard or long; then there is the catchall—god works in mysterious ways. On the other hand, if a prayer succeeds, we have no reason to ascribe that success to a supernatural being. Likewise, we have no reliable way to determine if the person who is giving testimony of his faith is truthful or fraudulent. We have no way of verifying the truthfulness of someone's claim that he or she has received a revelation, command, or a direction from god. God usually doesn't talk— we don't know if it doesn't talk, could not talk, or is just too busy to talk. Finally, miracles, as we have mentioned elsewhere in this book, are not reliable either. Religion doesn't allow us to evaluate the veracity of religious leaders as their teachings are either patently ambiguous or deal with an afterlife which is not accessible to experimentation and verification. Those who claim that they are born again Christians and that god will take them to heaven after their death, cannot be disputed; there is no way to subject those claims to scientific scrutiny. Any fraudulent, delusional, or serious believer could make those claims, as they are beyond verification. In reality, it doesn't matter what people profess to believe. Their actions prove their true beliefs.

If a scientist proposed the existence of heaven and hell, other scientists, if they thought the proposition was reasonable and worth pursuing, would start designing experiments to verify the existence of such places. The heat from the furnaces of hell would be scientifically verifiable. Scientists might put forward a hypothesis about the type of electromagnetic radiation that is likely to be emitted from a heaven or a hell. If collected data did not support their existence, the original hypothesis would be shelved. It should be relatively easy to disprove the existence of heaven, at least a heaven like Christians and Muslims envision. If people have bodily gone to heaven as is believed, food, oxygen, and clothing stores must be there. If those young Muslim men were to have 72 virgins available, there should be a big order of beds that could be traced. Also heaven would need to be within earth's atmosphere, as human life cannot exist in outer space – unless there is a big spaceship out there. Since so many people believe in heaven and since no one can prove there is no heaven, then according to common belief, there must be one.

Religion has an obligation to prove the existence of heaven, hell, gods, angels, spirits, and dancing virgins. But in fact, the very questioning of such concepts is discouraged and even punished. If one exhibits doubts about a doctrine, then one is not a believer and cannot belong to that religion.

While doubt and skepticism is the foundation of the scientific method, unquestioned faith and belief is the foundation of religion. Here lies the intractable difference between science and religion. We daresay, it is here that religion continues to lose ground because its beliefs continue to be exposed as faulty as the study of nature progresses. This is why evangelical Christians continue to challenge science while the scientists quietly go about their way pushing out the frontiers of knowledge.

The scientific method is important in our day-to-day lives. The physician, the scientist, as well as other individuals struggle to differentiate correlation from causality. The occurrence of two things close together does not mean that the first event is the cause of the second event. Many of the stories of miraculous events are based on this error.

Many people believe that science is too complicated to understand. However, we use the scientific method in our lives every day. If we put our hand on a stove, we realize that the stove is hot and we experience a burning sensation – that is knowledge. Knowledge is science. Knowledge is obtained by trial and error or by carefully designed experimentation. The learning process between birth and death is a continuum. In the process we find the more we know the more we realize how little we know. We as individuals cannot master the totality of truth but we can strive to attain some of it in our lives.

Life is a laboratory. Life is a constant experiment. The scientific method recognizes that emotions do not make truth. Strong faith or powerful preaching does not establish truth nor does it create wisdom. Dreams do not make reality nor do fantasies or illusions. Only facts with repeated testing establish truth. Unless a decision is absolutely necessary, it is wise to reserve judgment until as many facts as possible are known.

Some of our cherished myths are wrong. For example, both logic and emotion come from the brain, not from the heart, as many were taught. The idea that emotions come from the heart was the result of the mistaken religious belief that the heart was the residence of emotions and the seat of the soul. We now know quite conclusively that the heart is simply a pump and has no feelings or thoughts. With today's knowledge of anatomy and physiology and with our understanding of the brain, even though limited, we must conclude that if there is a soul, it must reside in the brain. Sometimes, however, myths are too powerful to be replaced by knowledge!

Our legislative bodies should realize that every law they enact is an experiment. There should be a big sign on the wall of every legislative chamber, "Don't Forget the Law of Unintended Consequences." Many laws are ineffective, expensive, or unenforceable — that means the experiment was a failure. Legislators, like all of us, should learn from their failures. Many laws fail because they are poorly worded wish lists and are vague and fail to define their terms. Good examples are laws to help the handicapped or laws mandating clean air or clean water that do not define their terms or give adequate parameters. Handicapped is now being interpreted by the courts to include gluttony, obesity, addictions, neuroses, and phobias – even allergies to peanuts and perfumes. Businesses are required to spend millions, not only to accommodate those who have been handicapped by god, but also those who are handicapped by their own design.

Our courts often fail to define their terms. The Supreme Court recently ruled that it is unconstitutional to execute the mentally retarded. That will give employment to hundreds of lawyers until the Supreme Court adequately defines mentally retarded. Legislators and judges should remember Edmund Burke's admonition that you must define your terms before you discuss an issue.

The Federal government should understand that laws are experiments and that the smaller and simpler the test, the easier it is to adjust and make changes in those laws. The Federal government should allow the states to do experimentation at the state level. If Oregon wants to try euthanasia, let it – then evaluate the results. It may turn out to be one of the most humane things that can be done for a suffering person as well as being economically wise for the family and society. If a state wants to decriminalize the usage of marijuana, let it. If the slippery slope theory holds true and gross abuses occur, it will be easier to correct at the state level than at the Federal level. The Federal Government needs to allow experimentation with the smallest numbers of people possible before instituting untried programs for the entire country.

Life is an experiment. Evaluate the results of your experience. Don't be afraid of science because you don't understand Einstein's theory of relativity. Science is neither moral nor immoral. It is neither bad nor good. It is simply the most reliable method of searching for truth. It should be obvious to all that the cosmos is indifferent, even hostile to man and that man must study, evaluate, and improve upon nature for his own happiness and welfare. There are many things in nature that man cannot control. But to refuse to investigate the things that we can control, based on the premise that god wants to control them, is ludicrous. That belief keeps humanity in the Dark Ages.

Truth never comes into the world but like a bastard, to the ignominy of him that brought her forth.

John Milton

CLONING AND HUMAN EMBRYO RESEARCH

Cloning and human embryo research (genomic research) rank right up with abortion as one of society's most divisive emotional issues. Knowledge is and always will be a double-edged sword. All new technology including genomic research brings forth comfort, ease, and advantages. It also elicits fear and anxiety.

Cloning naturally happens during reproduction when two or more identical descendents (identical twins, for example) have genes, which they share from both parents. However, the term cloning generally refers to asexual reproduction where the offspring has identical genetic material from only one parent. Gardeners, for instance, clone when they grow plants from leaf or branch cuttings. Cloning also occurs in plants when they send out shoots or grow from roots.

Genomic research has been going on for years. We have been using such research and knowledge for generations as we attempted to develop plants that were pest resistant, drought resistant, increased nutritional value, and improved yields. We have used that knowledge to produce animals that were disease resistant, more fertile, healthier, increased milk production, leaner meat, run faster, and so on. Historically, men and women have chosen mates – or had mates chosen for them – who would strengthen and lengthen the lives of their offspring. But the issue recently came to the forefront when scientists from Scotland successfully cloned a sheep, Dolly. Dolly was the first mammal to be so reproduced and it became apparent that human cloning was no longer science fiction.

Cloning research is closely related to embryo research—specifically, research on embryonic stem cells. Stem cell research attempts to understand the process in which undifferentiated embryonic cells become specialized cells that give rise to different organs in the body. Cloning will allow people to perpetuate their genetic makeup into future generations.

Genomic research has a number of potential benefits. These include:

- To grow whole organs that can be used to replace those that are diseased.
- To advance the understanding of cancer.
- To create animals that can produce medically beneficial materials.

- To understand the genetic basis of human and animal psychology, physiology, and anatomy.
- To study and treat conditions such as Parkinson's disease, heart disease, and paralysis due to spinal cord injuries.
- To develop a better understanding of drugs and aid in the development of specific, effective drugs.
- To extend human life.
- To identify and treat genetic diseases.

The research on embryos thus has the potential to ease the suffering from genetic abnormalities, cancer, Alzheimer's disease, Tay-Sachs, and sickle cell anemia; replace damaged cells in the heart, pancreas, central nervous system, and other organs. Human embryo research is very likely to alleviate human suffering.

But in the minds of those who believe that god is in control of all life, cloning research cannot be separated from such issues as the beginning of life, contraception, abortion, and in-vitro fertilization. Many religious people assert that life begins when an egg is fertilized and they want to treat every fertilized egg as a human being. They fail to realize that both the sperm and the egg were alive before they got together. They are appalled that humans are dabbling in an area previously reserved for god—the creation of life and the determination of what happens to that life. Until now, only god was capable of cloning life—though presumably Jesus was an example of a human born out of asexual reproduction. Now, not only god, but also humans are involved in the process of asexual reproduction. Thus the cry that man is playing god. (We won't open the bag of worms as to when the soul appears in human development.)

The slippery slope theory holds that research on human embryos will lead to all sorts of inhumane activities such as systematic genocides and murders. The critics of such research are afraid that parents will be able to design their children – the color of their eyes, their sex, and to free them from genetic abnormalities. The critics are afraid that fetuses with abnormalities will be aborted and they make the issue an emotional one by calling it "a culture of death".

Genomic research does raise many questions, along with much anxiety and fear. The medical, ethical, social, and legal issues, which will arise as the research continues, are formidable and are already being addressed. For example, is a fertilized egg outside of the human body "property" or "people"? The ethics and the laws that follow genomic research will be discussed and debated as the science emerges. Every new knowledge brings forth a whole new set of questions and problems, and genomic research will bring forth more than most, as god muddies the water in this discussion. Morality, ethics, and laws will as they always have, lag behind the accumulation of knowledge.

Some reproductive medical centers are already allowing parents to choose the sex of their child. Some couples are already choosing in-vitro fertilization, sperm and egg donation, and other artificial means to conceive. The boundaries continue to expand and will continue to expand over the objections of religions that claim, "God is running things just perfectly, thank you."

One must admit that any scientific research may be abused but the potential for abuse is not limited to genetic research. Thoughtful and well-debated laws and restrictions will be necessary to control those abuses. But to believe that man should not engage in cloning, stem cell, and other genetic research that has the potential for improving on nature, is inimical to our health and welfare.

There is the fear that the knowledge gained from genomic research will allow mankind to control its own evolution. That is a possibility. Certainly, humans controlling their own destiny will not be any more erratic or random than what has taken place through the natural process.

The religious establishment may be able to slow cloning and embryo research in the short run by maintaining that such research is against god's will, but it will not be successful in permanently stopping research from discovering cures, controlling diseases, and improving our life spans. Religion's concern that god is being continually diminished as researchers successfully delve deeper and deeper into nature's secrets, is an indication of the fundamental weakness of a theology that depends heavily on questionable concepts such as a virgin birth or a resurrection from the dead. It is theology that should adjust itself to advancing scientific progress; science has no obligation to shore up a faltering theology.

Historically, religious people have been against research, new ideas, and inventions as human advancement was seen as a diminishment of god. When man was experimenting with flight, the doomsayers said, "If god wanted man to fly it would have given him wings." But man succeeded in unlocking the secrets of flight even though he was not endowed with wings.

James Simpson, a British obstetrician, first used chloroform in 1847 to alleviate the pain of childbirth. He was attacked by the Church for interfering with god's desire for women to suffer in childbirth forever. Everyone who has read Genesis knows it is god's will for women to suffer in childbirth because Eve sinned in the Garden of Eden.

When Benjamin Franklin invented the lightning rod, the clergy criticized it as an attempt to defeat the will of god. The clergy in that day, and some even today believe that god uses lightning to punish sinners and that Franklin shouldn't have interfered with god's plans.

In a discussion of human embryo research we are in the same position we were when studying the smallpox virus. Some said then that god created smallpox and it knew what it was doing and thus man should not interfere with god's will.

Recently a woman with a strong family history of Alzheimer's disease was impregnated with a fertilized ovum that did not have the Alzheimer gene. Some medical ethicists and some clergy are upset about this as if god wants folks to develop Alzheimer's disease.

God regrettably did not create perfect embryos, children, adults, or even a perfect environment. Therefore, we must conduct research to deal with those imperfections. If god is to be given credit for life, then it must be held responsible for the large number of spontaneous abortions, malformed children, unwanted pregnancies, and the many problems and complications of reproduction and childbirth.

The claim that god did a perfect job with the reproductive process and that man should not improve upon it doesn't withstand scrutiny. God for instance puts new life into drug-addicted women's uteruses and aborts good parents' pregnancies. Miscarriages, which are god's abortions, end one third of all pregnancies. God, the creator of life, is increasing the human population at a rate that outstrips the world's ability to feed, clothe, and house them. Finally, god is indiscriminate in making parents. One wishes that god would know the difference between nurturing parents and those that are troubled, abusive, and murderous. God, like many humans, does not differentiate procreational from recreational sex.   Recreational sex produces children who are unwanted, neglected, and abused.   The religious teaching that god wants all fertilized eggs to develop into babies and that god loves them and will care for them is absurd.   That concept is a threat to a humane society.

God does not care about every fertilized human ovum as it allows and does nothing to prevent abnormal fetuses, congenital malformations, and the harmful environment in which children are born.   God's mistakes are flown into the United States from all over the world so that our surgeons can correct the malformed hearts, cleft palates, conjoined twins, and other congenital malformations. God does not treat every fertilized egg as a sacred life to be cherished and protected and neither should mankind.

Many objections were raised against in-vitro fertilization that allows infertile couples to have healthy children, instead of resigning them to a barren fate. It is now obvious that in-vitro fertilization is a needed and valuable service to parents and it is here to stay. Generally, the arguments against research on reproduction are based on fear.   First, there is the fear that man may create a monster.   This is a legitimate fear, as one can never predict the results of research.   However, man's deformed fetuses will not be any worse than god's.   Second, the politicians are afraid that they will lose the vote of the religious bloc if they support research on embryos and cloning. Many people believe that god's feelings will be hurt if such research is carried out and they don't want to hurt god's feelings. Third, there is the fear of a vengeful god who doesn't want anyone messing around with its plans, whatever those plans may be. Fourth, the manipulators and con men of religion are afraid that their livelihood is at risk as god becomes less and less relevant in the affairs of mankind. The fact that science can unite a sperm and an ovum in the test tube and keep it alive diminishes the need of a god but it doesn't diminish the need for more research. Finally, the theologians are fearful that they must give up some of their cherished beliefs and concede that man, not god, has created scriptures, revelations, and religious doctrines.

Let us assume that someone is standing at a street corner or at a church pulpit and addresses us in an emotional and charismatic voice:

> God doesn't want you to do research on hurricanes. God created hurricanes. God loves hurricanes. God wants hurricanes. Man should never, never try to change hurricanes. Hallelujah – Praise the Lord! But if you do research on hurricanes the wrath of the Lord will come down upon you and you will rot in hell for eternity. The Lord loves you. Hallelujah – Praise the Lord!

Most of us would ignore or laugh at such a person, but that is exactly what the religious right is saying about human embryo research and cloning.

We cannot predict the benefits or the harm of stem cell research, just as we could not predict the effects of fire, the wheel, or the atom bomb. That inability to predict the harmful effects of research has never stopped man from striving to improve upon nature. Most realize that every invention carries both beneficial and harmful consequences. After all, we can no longer live in comfort without electricity, but that same electricity can kill you.

Much of genetics rests upon risks and probabilities, both of which are used for predictions of the future. Most people do not understand or interpret risks and probabilities rationally, as emotions and feelings enter into their decisions. The risks of motor vehicle accidents vs. accidents on commercial airlines, attest to this – the risk of injury and death is far higher in motor vehicle accidents than in commercial airline accidents, but the widespread publicity of an airplane crash creates far more apprehension and fear than the commonplace motor vehicle accident. We can be certain that the risks and probabilities of genome research will be clouded by emotions, feelings, and irrationalities. But that will not stop inquisitiveness and inventiveness. Whether we like it or not, whether we do it intelligently or irrationally, we make many of life's decisions based upon risks and probabilities.

Those who wrote Genesis created a god who didn't want men and women to be inquisitive. In fact, we can argue that Eve is our first scientist, as her inquisitiveness and thirst for knowledge led to humanity's banishment from the Garden of Eden. If it were not for Eve, we would still be wandering around naked in the gardens and forests, living in caves, and eating raw flesh. Fortunately for all of us, Eve opened the gates of knowledge and god did not succeed in keeping us in the dark.

To question cloning and embryo research on the basis of human morality is legitimate. To question it on the basis of theology and god's alleged commandments is not. We should say to the researchers, "Full speed ahead. You must continue to improve upon nature's imperfect ways."

The true science and the true study of man is man.

Pierre Charron

HAPPINESS

The main reason to develop a personal philosophy is to become happy and content. Some of the beliefs of religion may contribute to happiness but a poorly communicating, jealous, vengeful god causes more fear than happiness. There are so many conflicting stories in religion that relatively few people can be certain that they meet god's requirements. The thousands of religions, sects, and gods, all with their own rules and requirements, attest to this. Some people know that all they have to do to get to heaven is to believe in Jesus Christ and accept him as their savior. Depending upon the strength of that belief, they may derive some happiness from it. On the other hand, those people who don't know if they believe in heaven or not, derive little satisfaction from the concept of immortality. Some others wait patiently for the arrival of a Messiah and do not believe that Jesus was that Messiah. Those believers obviously do not derive happiness from Christianity.

My advice to believers who cannot give up the rituals of their religion without guilt is to observe them as you would any superstition, then ignore them. If you want to practice those rituals lest you feel guilty, do so. Sprinkle holy water, take communion, cross yourself, go to confession, and then get on with your life. Most superstitious beliefs are not harmful.

Most people know in their minds and reveal by their actions that this life we live is all there is. Like the little boy who thinks he is going to heaven to be with his mother, he doesn't really believe it. He thinks it – he wishes for it – he may even say it, but he doesn't believe it.

The author may not be able to give you the secret of happiness but he can certainly give you the secret of unhappiness. Take all of today's problems, add yesterday's and tomorrow's, then you will have a recipe for misery. If you are capable of imagining a few problems that may occur in the future, you can develop a full-blown depression.

People seek happiness and truth. We seek truth because we must; happiness because it makes us feel better. People are unhappy for various reasons. There are too many causes to list in a book of this nature but it would be a good exercise for each individual to make a list of the causes of his or her unhappiness and then take a good look at them. You can best address your unhappiness if you know the cause of it. Even if the cause is unknown, one can frequently replace unhappiness with total involvement in work, play, family, or service. There is a saying that understanding a problem is ninety percent of the solution, so try to understand your unhappiness.

Albert Einstein's wife Elsa, when asked if she understood her husband's theory of relativity replied, "Oh no, although he has explained it to me many times – but it is not necessary for my happiness." That statement raises the question, "What is necessary for one's happiness?" Food, air, water, shelter, and safety are all necessary for survival and happiness. Hope, ability to love and be loved, and freedom from pain are also requirements for happiness. Many wish for an everlasting life, but it does not cause nor is it necessary for one's happiness on earth. A stern, unforgiving father figure who has created evil and hell, and a scorekeeper who keeps track of all of man's foibles will not provide happiness; it can only cause fear, misery, anger, and unhappiness. Boethius wrote in *Consolations of Philosophy* in 524 AD that happiness should be the aim of the wise.

Some simple rules for happiness follow. These may bother those who do not like platitudes and clichés but platitudes and clichés have universal appeal and carry kernels of truth. So skip them if you must, but adopt any that can give you some comfort and peace of mind. One just might help you get through some of the vicissitudes of life.

■   Don't sweat the little stuff.
If the stoplight turns red, waiting

a few more seconds is not really that important.

- It's just a matter of mind over matter – if you don't mind, it doesn't matter.
- Abe Lincoln said people are about as happy as they choose to be, so choose to be happy. Lincoln used this saying as well as humorous stories to relieve his depressions.
- Push your thoughts around; don't let your thoughts push you around.
- If life deals you a lemon, make lemonade.
- Adopt my favorite beatitude: "Blessed is he who expecteth nothing for he shall not be disappointed."
- Once when I was annoyed with my grandson, he looked me in the eye and said, "Lighten up, granddad." Good advice – lighten up!
- Bury yourself in work, play, or worthwhile activities.
- Hope for the best; prepare for the worst.
- Don't postpone joy. Take time to smell the roses.
- Do not overreact to minor slights or criticism. Don't allow your feelings to be easily hurt.

Enough with the clichés. Remember, your life belongs to you. It doesn't belong to god or to your neighbor.

John Galt, the hero in Ayn Rand's *Atlas Shrugged* said:

> For centuries, the battle of morality was fought between those who claimed that your life belongs to God and those who claimed that it belongs to your neighbors – between those who preached that the good is self-sacrifice for the sakes of ghosts in heaven and those who preached that the good is self-sacrifice for the sake of incompetents on earth. And no one came to say that your life belongs to you and that the good is to live it.

A Philosophy professor once asked his class, "Is life worth living?" A voice piped up from the back of the room, "What else can you do with it?" Strive to live life to its fullest.

There are two ways to attain happiness. You can determine what it takes to make you happy, then get it; or you can be happy with what you have. There are two reasons not to complain: first, it makes your friends sad; second, it makes your enemies happy. You don't want to do that to either of them.

Many times what happens to an individual is not as important as their reaction to it. The reaction to a slight or injury that should have been quickly forgotten or ignored has ruined many lives. That reaction can warp one forever. There is a high price to pay for hurt feelings. Many parents have ruined their children's lives by making a huge emotional issue out of something that should have been ignored or forgotten. Neither do parents help their children by making excuses for their misbehaviors, mistakes, and faulty judgments.

During my career in the Air Force we had frequent transfers during our children's growing up years. On those occasions I would read a book to them about a little girl who was soon to move from her familiar surroundings. The refrain at the end of each chapter was:

Keep an open heart,
Keep an open mind;
Look for the best,
And that's what you'll find.

Good advice for all.

Don't let yesterday use up too much of today.
Will Rogers

There is no duty we so much underrate as the duty of being happy.
Robert Louis Stevenson

The time to be happy is now.
The place to be happy is here.
The way to be happy is to try to make others so.
Speech by Robert G. Ingersoll -
"The Limitation of Toleration"

ENLIGHTENED SELF-INTEREST

Enlightened self-interest rather than religion must guide our actions. While religion attempts to guide us in the right direction by means of the carrot of heaven and the stick of hell, the concept of self-interest requires us to think what, why, and how we do things the way we do. As we look inward we recognize that we make mistakes and that it is necessary to own up to those mistakes and take corrective action. We also recognize that it is in our self-interest to be charitable and caring of our fellow man and our environment. We do not need priests, preachers, gods, commandments, churches, and out of this world conundrums to make us that way.

Jeremy Bentham, an eighteenth century English philosopher, coined the term "self regarding interest" to say that man does what he thinks is in his own interest. Bentham believed that the world was made up of people pursuing their own interests and pleasures, with the necessity of controlling others so that they would not interfere with those desires. He called upon law, religion, and public opinion to help attain the means to pursue our own interests. Individuals pursuing their own desires and pleasures must realize that they cannot ignore the interests of others to do the same.

The concept of enlightened self-interest underlies our adherence to a free market economy where all pursue their economic dream. A free and open market helps us achieve our goals.

Enlightened self-interest is different from raw selfishness. Selfishness is a pejorative word and describes self-centered, grabby, uncaring, mean people. Selfishness is not a desirable trait. However, all of us strive to meet our basic needs for food, clothing, heat, shelter, companionship, and family. Enlightened self-interest recognizes the necessity to meet our basic needs and the need to work together to satisfy them. Also, it is in our own self-interest to enable others to meet their needs. In that sense, enlightened self-interest in contrast to selfishness is a desirable trait and allows us to live peaceably within our local and global communities.

Enlightened self-interest lets us recognize that our own interest is best served by being aware of others and helping them to achieve their interests. Colin Powell acknowledged at the UN World Summit, "We have always understood that our well-being depends on the well-being of our fellow inhabitants of this planet Earth."

Man's environment encompasses not only his fellow man but also nature. The person who never bathes is part of our environment; the person who blows smoke in our faces is part of our environment. It is in our own enlightened self-interest to improve ourselves, and to improve others and the environment. We need not feel guilty for tending to our own interests as long as we are aware of other's and do not trample on their rights.

M. de Tocqueville writes in *On Democracy in America*:

> The principle of enlightened self-interest is not a lofty one; but it is clear and sure. It does not aim at mighty objects; but it attains, without impracticable efforts, all those at which it aims. As it lies within the reach of all capacities, every one can without difficulty apprehend and retain it. By its adaptation to human weakness, it easily obtains great dominion; nor is its dominion precarious, since it employs self-interest itself to correct self-interest; and uses, to direct the passions, the very instrument which excites them.
> The doctrine of enlightened self-interest produces no great acts of self-sacrifice; but it suggests daily small acts of self-denial. By itself it cannot suffice to make a virtuous man; but it disciplines a multitude

of citizens in habits of regularity,
temperance, moderation, foresight,
self-command; and, if it does not
at once lead men to virtue by their
will, it draws them gradually in that
direction by their habits.

Although de Tocqueville admirably
summarizes the notion of enlightened self-
interest, we must point out that it does produce
great acts of self-sacrifice as we have seen over
and over in our American democracy. In
America's brief history, thousands have given
their lives so that others may enjoy theirs.
Enlightened self-interest is a lofty goal and is
the best suited of all philosophies to ensure
the welfare of men and women. The principle
of enlightened self-interest is clear and sure.

When one worries about the public good,
that is enlightened self-interest. Peace and
security for the public is peace and security for
the individual. Justice and equity do not come
from an invisible, uncommunicative divine
power, but comes from man's efforts to be
treated fairly and justly.

Self-interest accounts for man's morality.
John Stuart Mill, a nineteenth century English
philosopher and economist, originated the term
"utilitarianism" to explain his theory that
actions are right in proportion as they tend to
produce happiness; wrong as they tend to
produce unhappiness. Utilitarianism, like
ethics, is enlightened self-interest. Perhaps
when people cease to work for an all-powerful,
all-knowing god they can spend more time on

their own welfare and the welfare of their fellow man.

The words of Eusebius, the Greek historian, 2000 years ago addresses modern day living better than any religion today:

> May I be no man's enemy and may I be the friend of that which is eternal and abides. May I never devise evil against any man; if any devise evil against me, may I escape. May I love, seek, and attain only that which is good. May I wish for all men's happiness and envy none. When I have done or said what is wrong, may I never wait for the rebuke of others, but always rebuke myself until I make amends. May I win no victory that harms either me or my opponent. May I reconcile friends who are wroth with one another. May I, to the extent of my power, give all needful help to all who are in want. May I never fail a friend in danger. May I respect myself. May I always keep tame that which rages within me. May I never discuss who is wicked and what wicked things he has done, but know good men and follow in their footsteps.

*Down in their hearts, wise men know this truth;
the only way to help yourself is to help others*
Elbert Hubbard

A Religious Bill of Rights

J ust as the United States Constitution established a Bill of Rights to protect its citizens, so should a Religious Bill of Rights be created to maintain peace and tranquility and allow the citizens of the world intellectual and religious freedom:

- No person shall be required to pray in public.
- Freedom from religion is a basic human right and religions must respect the right of individuals to have freedom from religion as well as freedom of religion.
- In no instance shall a person be required to express belief or disbelief in religious concepts such as the existence of god, heaven, hell, miracles, saints, angels, reincarnation, and so on.

■ All persons shall have the right to hold diverse religious and intellectual beliefs, free from the harm of others.

■ No religion will be allowed to preach or practice harmful concepts such as holy crusades, holy wars, jihads, fatwas, and other related activities that are based on the perception that killing nonbelievers will allow them entrance into heaven.

■ Religions are specifically prohibited from inciting their followers to perform hateful, harmful, or illegal activities in the name of their deity.

■ Religions are required to denounce, condemn, and repudiate any and all passages in their dogmas and scriptures which threaten the well-being of people who hold differing beliefs – pejorative words such as pagan, infidel, and unbeliever are prohibited.

■ No person shall be required to acknowledge or profess to believe in any dogma, creed, or god as a condition of employment, membership, or acceptance into any organization. Belief or non-belief may not be used as a requirement for receipt of any entitled benefit.

■ The right of the people to be free from unwanted evangelism and proselytism shall not be violated; freedom of expression and freedom of religion being the law of the land does not give others permission to exert that right on those who do not wish to receive it.

■ Human conduct being a function and responsibility of human beings, religions will not be permitted to advance their beliefs into the affairs of humanity. Rules, regulations, and laws will be enacted solely for the welfare of human beings without consideration of god's desires.

■ No sectarian tenets shall be taught in any school supported in whole or in part by public taxation.

■ Church and state will remain separate and distinct, each free to work within their own spheres.

■ The enumeration in the above Religious Bill of Rights shall not be construed to deny or disparage other rights retained by the people.

If these rights are recognized and honored, far fewer conflicts would exist.

CONCLUSION

For the thinking, reasonable, logical person there is no man-like god who is consciously, intelligently running the universe. Religions and gods have caused untold conflicts, wars, and hatred without establishing a worthwhile moral code on which humanity can agree. Good people will remain good with or without religions and gods. Bad people will continue to use religion to convince others to do their bidding and to justify their own actions. A troubled world demands that we reevaluate religion's claim on morality.

This book tries to give comfort to those who question the concept of an all-powerful, all-knowing, all-righteous being who stands by quietly while humanity suffers. It tries to ease the guilt and fear of those who were frightened in childhood with a god who would send them to hell if they did not believe and obey their religious leader. It attempts to make religion kinder, more tolerant, and more humane. Lastly, these writings can give courage to those who would speak out and criticize religion when it is inimical to mankind's well-being.

Humanism, the concept that humanity must be responsible for its own actions, morality, well-being, and environment, must replace theism if mankind is to prosper and live in peace.

The world comes to those who think; tragedy to those who feel.

Horace Walpole

RECOMMENDED BOOKS

Adler, Mortimer J. *How to Think About God: A Guide for the 20ᵗʰ Century Pagan.* New York: Macmillan, 1980.

Armstrong, Karen. *The Battle for God.* New York: Alfred Knopf, 2000.

Blaker, Kimberly. *The Fundamentals of Extremism: The Christian Right in America.* New Boston Books, 2003.

Funk, Robert W. and Roy W. Hoover and the Jesus Seminar. *The Five Gospels: The Search for the Authentic Words of Jesus.* New York: Macmillan, 1993. Reprint: San Francisco: Harper San Francisco, 1997.

Funk, Robert W. and the Jesus Seminar. *The Acts of Jesus: The Search for the Authentic Deeds of Jesus.* San Francisco: Harper San Francisco, 1998.

Hoffer, Eric. *The True Believer: Thoughts on the Nature of Mass Movements.* New York: Perennial, 2002.

Ingersoll, Robert. *On the Gods and Other Essays.* Buffalo: Prometheus Books, 1990)

Kemelman, Harry. *Conversations With Rabbi Small.* New York: Morrow, 2003.

Lamont, Corliss. *The Philosophy of Humanism.* 7ᵗʰ ed. New York: Continuum, 1990.

Moreland, James Porter and Kai Neilsen. *Does God Exist?: The Debate Between Theists and Atheists.* Nashville, TN: T. Nelson, 1990. Reprint: Buffalo: Prometheus Books, 1993.

Paine, Thomas. *Age of Reason.* New York: Wiley, 1989.

Raymo, Chet. *Skeptics and True Believers: The Exhilarating Connection Between Science and Religion.* New York: Walker & Co., 1998.

Russell, Bertrand. *On God and Religion.* Buffalo: Prometheus Books, 1986.

Russell, Bertrand. *Why I Am Not a Christian.* New York: Simon & Schuster, 1957.

Sagan, Carl. *The Demon-Haunted World: Science As a Candle in the Dark.* New York: Random House, 1995. Reprint: Ballantine Books, 1997.

Seckel, Al, ed. *Bertrand Russell on God and Religion.* Buffalo: Prometheus Books, 1986.

Spong, John Shelby. *Rescuing the Bible from Fundamentalism: A Bishop Rethinks the Meaning of Scripture.* San Francisco: Harper San Francisco, reprint 1992.

Spong, John Shelby. *Why Christianity Must Change or Die: A Bishop Speaks to Believers In Exile.* San Francisco: Harper San Francisco, 1999.

Strobel, Lee. *The Case for Faith: A Journalist Investigates the Toughest Objections to Christianity.* Grand Rapids, MI: Zondervan Publishing House, 2000.

Wilson, Harry. *Freedom from God: Restoring the Sense of Wonder.* Albuquerque: Amador Publishers, 2002.

WHAT THE READERS SAY ABOUT
FEAR FAITH FACT FANTASY

Few people have helped and at times forced me to think as deeply and clearly as John Henderson does. This book is another example of his sharp and insightful mind, caring heart, and humorous personality.

Rev. Roy L. Hood, Retired Southern Baptist and United Methodist Minister, who is also a Quaker

John Henderson's new book comes from his heart because he dwells in the real house of the Lord. He claims to be a Humanist-Atheist, whatever that might be, but having known him for many years, he is unquestionably a spiritual person who sees through the fog and fraud of organized religion. This book shows the hypocrisy of a male-dominated man-made god in all his shallowness.

Peter Allen Gentling, M.D., Poet, Painter, Gardener, and student of the Buddha

At last we have a definitive study of the fallacy of religion – the first complete inquiry into the beliefs that have hampered man in his search for truth. Dr. Henderson's book can change the world.

Susan Dart, author of Market Square

"Here I stand, I can do no other," was Martin Luther's response when his conscience and thinking came into conflict with what he was asked to believe based on some one else's authority. John Henderson takes a similarly principled stand in Fear Faith Fact Fantasy, though the place he ends up standing is a bit different from Martin Luther's. Henderson raises arguments against the run of the mill way most people think about God and presents them in a witty, accessible, and provocative way. He argues that religion does more harm than good. Like Luther's, his views will both annoy and seem like common sense. Do not read this book unless you are willing to think for yourself.

Theodore M. Vial, Jr., Ph.D., Associate Professor of Religious Studies, Virginia Wesleyan College

Fundamentalism is on the rise. As a father of four, I fear that the rise of intolerant religion will lead to Armageddon as the Bible states. Dr. Henderson proposes a universal humanism based on thought, not faith. If people were to follow his ideas, there is hope for future generations.

Steve Kovach, M.D.

Can proprietary notions of god and religion survive globalization? Will emerging science faze religious fervor into rational humanism? Fear Faith Fact Fantasy forces the reader to meet such moral challenges head-on.

Frankie Schelly, author of At the Crossroads,
2002 DIY Fiction Winner

With the writing of FEAR FAITH FACT FANTASY, John A. Henderson, M.D. presents a thoughtful consideration of "that ole time religion" in a twenty-first century world. Are some of our present day dilemmas exacerbated because we are philosophically enrolled in a harsher code of behavior by the teaching of many of our major religious congregations? The questions posed in Henderson's book serve as guideposts for critical assessment of the place and stance of philosophical thought today. The author obviously delights in Socratic argument and entices us to join the fray.

Betty Maxwell Daniel, Orlando, Florida

In FEAR FAITH FACT FANTASY, Dr. Henderson has plumbed the depths of the world religions and measured them against what can be proved and what can never be proved. The chapter on Faith is particularly thought provoking. After years of my own questions, Dr. Henderson has only strengthened my own answers.

Bonnie Habel, Author of Nevr, Nevr, Never Quit

In FEAR FAITH FACT FANTASY, Dr. Henderson has written a common sense book on belief and unbelief. He gives us many insights and thoughts which make the Christian god - and all other conventional gods - impossible. Merely to think along with John will make us see there is no Great Good Spirit in the heavens

226

running the universe. In this new book he goes a step further to show how a good, ethical, democratic society can be an atheistic society. Common sense tells us it doesn't do to ask what Jesus would do, or "would he drive an SUV?" Evolution and the environment are finite and require good ethical action. "Multiply and subdue the earth" may have been good advice for the primitive herdsmen who wrote the Bible, but for modern society the imperatives have changed. Simple thought and common sense tell us that there are no miracles and that we must shape our own ethics and rules for life.

Wolf Roder, Professor of Geography
University of Cincinnati, Ohio

Don't read this book if you aren't prepared to think. Dr. John A. Henderson's FEAR FAITH FACT FANTASY is not a book for the lazy mind. Agree or disagree, you are in for a mental romp.

Jack R. Pyle, author of award winning novel
The Sound of Distant Thunder.

Filled with insightful and provocative comments, Henderson's FEAR FAITH FACT FANTASY should be a required reading for all humanists and skeptics who are always on the lookout for writers who can also entertain as they educate and inform. In this book, Henderson gives attention to the paradoxes and implausibilities found in every aspect of the concept and definition of God and his powers. Quite clearly, in Henderson's words, "The concept of God is a human invention. That is why we have so many religions, mythologies, and systems of belief."

Robert A. Baker, Ph. D., Professor Emeritus,
Department of Psychology, University of Kentucky

WHAT SOME CRITICS HAVE SAID

Oy, vey! Such a terrible book

Rabbi U.R. Chosen
Beth Israel Synagogue, NYC

I shall enjoy looking over the wall of heaven and watching the author of this drivel suffer for eternity, if not longer.

Pious the 48th, Roma, Italia

May God have mercy on this poor, miserable, unenlightened, blasphemous soul. I shall pray that he will see the truth

The Most Reverend I.M. Wright
Seventh Baptist Church, Chicago, Illinois

This is without a doubt the worst book I have ever had the misfortune to read.

Dr. I.D. Clare, Editor
Christian Views

What a waste of time, effort, and trees

The Honorable I.C. Nada, Chairman,
Forest Protection Committee

Boy, is this guy full of it.

Dr. Kelog Awbran, Proctologist

May the horse of Muhammad kick Henderson in the head

Imam Komeany
Terrorran, Iran

Once you pick up this book you will never be able to put it down fast enough.

I.B. Fast, Editor, Religion for Dummies

You have never read anything like this before and you will never want to read anything like it again.

I.M. Shure, Professor of Catholic Studies,
SMU, Dallas, Texas

ABOUT THE BOOK:
FEAR FAITH FACT FANTASY

September 11, 2001 shocked the entire world as millions watched airplanes crash into the World Trade Center killing thousands of innocent women, men, children, Jews, Christians, Muslims, Buddhists, and Atheists – all in the name of god.

All had to wonder what the role of god, satan, or fate was in this tragedy. As people considered the gods, religions, and beliefs – past and present – they turned inward to contemplate their own god. This has caused many to question the relevance of god in the affairs of humanity.

This book dares the reader to think and reason logically on even the existence of god, let alone its involvement in human affairs. The harm of religion is stressed along with a plea for all to speak out when religion is used to express intolerance, hatred, and bigotry. If your religion has become too narrow, irrelevant, or outdated, this book is a must. All who have struggled with religion and questioned its teachings will benefit from the intellectual exercise of considering the author's ideas.

This book can relieve anxiety over doubts about religion; it can relieve guilt over your failure to live up to other's beliefs; it can ease the fear of an all-powerful, all-knowing god; and finally it can give people the courage to speak out against bigotry and intolerance as expressed by the various religions.

Henderson is writing what many think but are afraid to say.

Humanism, not theism, will be the savior of mankind.

About the Author

John A. Henderson, M.D. is a retired Air Force Flight Surgeon and General Surgeon. He is now a semi-retired General Surgeon living in Asheville, North Carolina with his wife Ruth. They have three children: Robert, Christine, and Jeanne. Henderson graduated with honors from the University of Illinois College of Medicine in 1945. He interned at the Research and Educational Hospital, Chicago, Illinois; his surgical residency was at Scott and White Clinic, Temple, Texas.

During his Air Force career, he served in England, Spain, and Japan, as well as various stateside assignments from New York to California. Dr. Henderson and his wife have traveled extensively, both in the Air Force and in civilian life.

The views which Dr. Henderson espouses have been with him since early childhood. He welcomes your views and comments. He can be reached via e-mail at: *jrh828@webtv.net*

Index